Trust and integrity
in the global economy

Michael Smith

Caux Books
in association with
Caux Initiatives for Business

First published 2007 by
Caux Books
in association with
Caux Initiatives for Business

Caux Books
Rue de Panorama
1824 Caux
Switzerland

also available from:
Initiatives of Change, 24 Greencoat Place, London SW1P 1RD

A CIP catalogue record for this book is available from the British Library.

ISBN   978-2-88037-516-4

Typesetting and text design in 10.5 Palatino by Blair Cummock
Cover design by Hayden Russell

Printed and bound by Impress Print Services
10 Thornsett Road, London SW18 4EN, UK
www.impressprint.net

Contents

Foreword - 1

I AM glad that Michael Smith has brought together this collection of stories. They illustrate how economic and social entrepreneurs, public sector service providers, farmers, educators, charity workers and society activists play their part in helping to meet the UN's Millennium Development Goals. These goals include halving the number of people living in absolute poverty and providing universal primary education for all by 2015. The stories especially emphasise the commitment to personal moral, spiritual and ethical motivations. There is a grain of love that the Creator has planted in each one of us. It is up to us to help this grain to grow or we can bury it for ever. These stories speak of care and selflessness, the courageous stance against corruption and deep concern for the environment. The stories also emphasise the need for building relationships of trust so essential if the MDGs are to be met. This book reflects the spirit of Initiatives of Change (IofC), that we see at work in the Caux centre, in Switzerland, and Asia Plateau, the Asian centre in Panchgani, India. I am therefore very happy to commend highly this useful book.

Mohamed Sahnoun
President, IofC International, and Special Advisor
to the Secretary-General of the United Nations

Trust and integrity
in the global economy

Foreword - 2

IN ANCIENT times—before the rise of the organization cubicle—the heroism of individuals was taken for granted as a standard for personal excellence.

Think of Odysseus between Scylla and Charybdis, Anaeas bearing his father out from flaming Troy, Caesar surrounding the Gauls in Alesia, Cicero's Phillpics against Antony, Confucius's call for high character. But today a spiritual drudgery inculcated by a need to toe the line and fit in to team cultures claims first place in our work lives—to get along by going along.

Michael Smith has written an important book challenging the need to succumb to this modern mental slavery, describing some who are leaders, not followers. His conclusions as to what it takes to make a difference are reassuring because the skills he finds necessary are readily at hand for all of us.

Stephen B Young
Global Executive Director
Caux Round Table
www.cauxroundtable.org

Trust and integrity in the global economy

AN EAST African trainee teacher says he has been cheated out of his income. As part of his degree course he gave 26 hours tuition in maths and business studies to students at a private school—but his employer paid him only $12, about a quarter of what he was owed. There was no written contract and he thought it was an agreement based on trust. Now he feels betrayed. In future, he comments, he will have 'a hard time trusting private investors. It was very painful but deep in my heart I resolve that I will take my experience positively and continue with life.'

He tells this story during a workshop on 'ethical leadership in business', billed for those setting out on the start of their careers, at a conference on business values held in Caux, Switzerland, in August 2006.

The six-day conference brought together an eclectic group of business professionals, farmers active with an international Farmers' Dialogue, and journalists involved in a media ethics campaign called the International Communications Forum.

The student teacher takes heart from the anti-corruption stance of Kenyan lawyer Joseph Karanja, who founded a legal practice in Nairobi in 1998 to 'send a message that lawyers too can be trustworthy'. His firm of eight lawyers has become well known for fighting corruption cases for business people 'who are willing to stand for the truth', he says, rather than pay bribes to corrupt officials in Nairobi city council. 'We have never lost a case but the city council has suffered huge losses by compensating our clients as a result of malicious prosecutions,' Karanja says. 'We have won over 40 corruption cases in the last four years. Today, Nairobi city council will drop a case before it goes to court, when they realise that we will be defending it.'

This means a loss of income for his firm but it has been worth it. 'There is no doubt,' he says, 'that there has been a turning point in the war against corruption in Kenya', despite the fact that Kenya's anti-corruption tsar, John Githongo, was driven overseas by death threats. 'We have had radical surgery in the judiciary,' Karanja says. 'The Chief Justice and 12 out of the 16 high court judges were sacked in 2004, as well as 378 magistrates implicated in corruption. Several ministers of the new government, who were perceived to be untouchable, were hounded out of office.'[1]

Blair Cummock

Jamshed Irani

Jamshed Irani, a director on the parent board of the giant Indian conglomerate Tata, tells the conference that he finds little in the West's emphasis on 'corporate social responsibility' that the Tata group hasn't been practising for nearly a century. The company pioneered the world's first eight-hour working day in 1912; free medical aid for employees in 1915; leave with pay in 1920; maternity benefit in 1928; the list goes on, all introduced decades before they became mandatory under law. When militant Maoists started attacking businesses in West Bokaro, near the Tata city of Jamshedpur, Tata Steel's coal mining base was untouched because, claims Irani, local people put out the word, 'Don't disturb Tatas'. The company was, after all, looking after the community, supplying water, medical aid and doctors to several hundred thousand people. 'We cannot remain spikes of prosperity in a sea of poverty,' Irani comments.

'The end never, never justifies the means,' Irani declares, describing how the managing director of one Tata company had been summarily sacked, prosecuted and jailed after he grossly breached Tata's code of conduct. 'Values essentially provide us with an internal discipline. Values transmit trust. Trust is not only at the heart of leadership but forms the essence of all relationships.' India, which 200 years ago claimed 20 per cent of world trade, was now re-emerging on the world stage, with annual growth rates of over eight per cent, second only to China.

Irani deplored as 'a disaster' the current emphasis on short-term, quarterly results, which pander to shareholders. In this he is echoed by Professor Paul Dembinski, Director of the Geneva-based Observatoire de la Finance, who says that the focus on short-term dividends, rather than future generations, gives more importance to capital than to employment. Financial speculation has too often become 'mass gambling', sometimes breaking businesses and destroying jobs.

Journalists too tend to pander to the market, says South African journalist Guy Berger. They too easily 'hide behind the "ethics" of getting the story at any cost'—including lying, stealing and intruding on grieving families—in order to give their audiences and readers what they want. 'Shouldn't the media be leading the market', by covering stories which address such issues as poverty? Berger, who was the 2006 recipient of the Nat Nakaski award for integrity and bravery in journalism, speaks from hard-won experience: his stance against apartheid earned him three years in jail and five years in exile.

The conference title contains a certain *double-entendre*: can individuals live in a spirit of trust and integrity within the global economy? And can the global economy be trusted to deliver justice and prosperity for all the world's citizens?

Canadian economist Genevieve LeBaron doubts it. 'Those who write about economic globalization as an unambiguously positive phenomenon are not telling the whole story,' she says. As an 18-year-old serving in an orphanage in Madras (now Chennai) in south India, she passed a factory where 'young girls sat in shrivelling heat from sunrise to sunset, dipping their bare hands in toxic chemicals, piecing computer parts together. I wondered then, how are these girls benefitting from this globalized world?' That same day, Tamil Nadu state farmers crowded

11

Madras's streets, protesting against an American corporation that was trying to patent their variety of rice.

Both situations may well have since been outlawed. But LeBaron deplores a situation that systematically excludes people, 'sometimes entire regions', from the marketplace. 'We need to question our society's conception of growth and progress,' she says. What would it take to 'shift the distributive dynamics of the global economy, to close the exponentially increasing gap in material wealth? Are we simply working towards making ourselves materially richer? What would we need to change about ourselves and the global economy to create a world in which all human beings can flourish?'

Blair Cummock

Genevieve LeBaron

The questions are left hanging in the air. But the issues won't go away. The farmers at the conference give dire warnings about the effects that global warming, climate change and population growth will have on agricultural output. Water shortages will be rife, for instance. 'Global water consumption is doubling every 20 years,' says Farmers' Dialogue leader Jim Wigan. 'By the year 2025, 48 countries are expected to face chronic water shortages affecting 2.8 billion people.' There is concern that Western farm subsidies are depriving developing world growers of their markets, though Europe's Common Agricultural Policy is being cut back. And anyway, says Wigan, with global population growth the world is going to need all the food production possible.

Christiane Lambert, the first woman president of a French farmers' union, insists that no farmer feels happy with having to survive on subsidies. But she is equally concerned about the 'psychological trauma' that French farmers face in complying with 200 European Union directives, the breach of any one of which causing loss of income. She pleads for 'a logic of sustainable development', rather than 'liberal fundamentalism' in trade, and an urgent reopening of the Doha development round of negotiations at the World Trade Organization.

For the young entrepreneurs and activists setting out on their careers, the global perspectives provide a challenging context for their decision making and priorities. As the East African student teacher comments, 'I am ready to be an instrument of change wherever I may be.' Conference co-organiser Joe Swann, working then for a service company in London helping the long-term unemployed back into jobs, is also challenged. 'Here I have met people who are not just living to work, but working to live,' he says. It has left him reflective on his priorities. Working to performance criteria may be good business practice but can be pressuring, he says, if it means skimping on the needs of his clients in order to show results. 'I will never, never undermine the interests of the individuals I work with to pursue personal gain or promotion.'

It all boils down to care for people, says Boston-based Ward Vandewege, a sole proprietor in software and information technology services. With customers in five countries, he has to deliver on trust and integrity if he is to compete globally. 'You have to demonstrate reliability. You have to care for your customers. The relationship of trust that you build up with your customer is essential for your business to survive. I know 90 per cent of my customers personally. I need to get to know them in order to build mutual trust. And you know what? I am happy about that. I think it makes life much more interesting.'

1. See also Joseph Karanja's story, chapter 8, page 69.

1

A scar on the conscience of the world

WHAT, then, are the great issues that confront the generation growing up in the foothills of the 21st century? Terrorism and its causes, of course, and relations between Islam and the West, but also the gap between the world's rich and poor, and the environmental destruction that exacerbates global warming and increases poverty—often fuelled by the naked greed of western consumerism.

In his book *An Inconvenient Truth*, former US Vice-President and Nobel laureate Al Gore writes that the climate crisis 'offers us the chance to experience what very few generations in history have had the privilege of knowing: *a generational mission*; the exhilaration of a compelling *moral purpose*; a shared and unifying cause; the thrill of being forced by circumstances to put aside the pettiness and conflict that so often stifle the restless human need for transcendence; *the opportunity to rise*' [his italics]. He goes on to describe this as 'a moral and spiritual challenge'[1].

The same could be said of the struggle to alleviate extreme poverty. Nearly a billion people live on less than a dollar a day—the UN's definition of absolute poverty. 'Can anyone doubt that this is the greatest moral challenge facing humankind?' asks the columnist and Oxford professor Timothy Garton Ash[2].

'The poorest of the poor in the world—and this includes poor people in prosperous societies—are going to be the worst hit' by climate change and rising global temperatures, predicts

Rajendra Pachauri, Chairman of the UN's Intergovernmental Panel on Climate Change. 'People who are poor are least able to adapt to climate change,' he said at the launch of the panel's report in April 2007. Up to 250 million people in African countries are projected to be the worst hit by drought and crop failures, says the report.[3]

Some of today's generation—politicians and campaigners, entrepreneurs, educators and economists, artists and actors, journalists, broadcasters, film-makers, musicians and many more—will determine to change things. They will scale the Himalayan heights to create an alternative future. Not everyone will, of course, and those who remain in the foothills also provide valuable service from base camp. But what does it mean to have a calling—to give one's life for a great cause? What are the implications? And what are the qualities needed? The stories in this book, taken largely from the entrepreneurial field, serve as illustrations of such a determination to make a difference, to change the world.

The world is already changing far more rapidly than most of us might have imagined at the outset of the century. By the 2050s, China and India will be major economic superpowers. China is expected to be the world's biggest economy measured by GDP, bouncing the USA into second place, with India third. By then, India will have the world's largest population. 'The world is being remade for all of us,' commented the BBC's diplomatic correspondent, James Robbins, in reports from India and China in July 2006.[4] David Smith, the Economics Editor of *The Sunday Times*, London, writes that the two countries are 'the biggest thing to hit the global economy and the most effective anti-poverty programme the world has ever seen'.[5] India's Prime Minister, Manmohan Singh, says: 'Together India and China can reshape the world.'[6]

Yet rural and urban poverty continues to afflict both countries, as it does in much of Africa. Anyone from the West who has lived in a developing country is never likely to forget their first sight of grinding poverty in the midst of affluence. I was 24 years old when I travelled to India for the first time in 1971 and was surprised not by the poverty, which I had been led to expect, so much as by the wealth: the Manhattan skyline of downtown Bombay cheek by jowl with the shanty huts and squalor. Perhaps I should not have been so surprised by the wealth. But this was two decades before the economic liberalizations brought in by Manmohan Singh, then Finance Minister, in the early 1990s.

Now renamed Mumbai, the 'city of dreams'—the world's most densely populated city[7]—has included Asia's largest slum in the suburb of Dharavi. But Singh, Prime Minister since 2004, insists that Mumbai will become 'India's Shanghai'.

India's wealth creation is thriving, with annual growth exceeding eight per cent—second only to China's 10 per cent. China's huge growth rates—and her trade surplus with the United States—are fuelled by her entrepreneurial spirit and global sales of consumer goods produced in her low wage economy. India is barking at China's heels. The two countries are in a tortoise and hare race to be the world's largest economy—inconceivable 50 years ago. Yet, as David Smith points out, they are returning to a position of pre-eminent wealth. Two thousand years ago India and China between them accounted for nearly 60 per cent of the global economy and, as recently as 1820, as much as 49 per cent, compared with Western Europe's 24 per cent. In speech after speech, Gordon Brown has repeatedly referred to 'the challenges of India and China'.

With a middle class of 300 million, India is said to have 100 million people, a tenth of the population, with an income higher than the average European. But India also has 40 per cent of the world's poorest people, and the second largest HIV population.[8]

Those in the West who have never travelled to the developing world have become accustomed to images of abject poverty on their TV screens. Many have campaigned vigorously to alleviate the suffering by supporting aid agencies and rock concerts such as Live Aid and Live 8. Celebrities led by Bono and Bob Geldof kept the need to tackle global poverty on the world's agenda. The Make Poverty History campaign of 2005, and its American counterpart, One, resulted in the world's largest ever petition. This had a major impact on the G8 summit of world leaders in Gleneagles, Scotland, in July that year, pushing for debt relief and increased aid. And in July 2007 Live Earth concerts in eight cities around the world highlighted environmental concerns.

Causes of poverty

The appalling gap between the world's rich and poor has been exacerbated by insurmountable mountains of debt, unfair and self-interested trade relationships, Western farm subsidies and protectionism, the greed of western consumerism, corruption and poor governance.

Some commentators, such as the Nobel Prize-winning economist Joseph Stiglitz, say that poverty was made worse by the punitive structural adjustment programmes demanded of developing countries by the West in return for financial support. Too many countries suffered from a rushed privatization and liberalization of their economies, without an adequate 'sequencing' of the process to protect them from international competition.[9] At the same time, rich countries have too often acted hypocritically in urging developing countries to open their markets whilst protecting their own.

For the British business consultant John Carlisle, 'the real scandal is the international debt that has dragged poor countries into a monetary equivalent of a master-servant culture.' Some progress towards writing off developing countries' debts has been made, thanks to the pressure on governments from grassroots campaigns such as the Jubilee Debt Campaign, but not nearly far enough. Twenty-two highly indebted poor countries had their debts written down following the Gleneagles summit, but other countries who have serviced their debts regularly—and remained creditworthy—have not seen their debts cancelled, and feel cheated.[10]

Prabhat Kumar, the Director of an independent Centre for Governance in New Delhi, and former Cabinet Secretary, insists that many developing countries also suffer from a 'palpable crisis of governance' of their own making.[11]

17

The scandal today

Above all, it is an affront to human dignity that millions around the world still live today, in a world of plenty, without their basic needs being met—for food, health, shelter, clothing, and education. This is one of the great moral issues of the early 21st century. Former Prime Minister Tony Blair described it as 'a scar on the conscience of humanity'[12].

It is also arguable that the world's gross injustices—including the juxtaposition of poverty and affluence—fuel the anger, alienation and humiliation that give rise to terrorism. 'To fight terrorism we will need to fight poverty and deprivation as well,' writes the American economist Jeffrey Sacks. 'We need to address the underlying weaknesses of the societies in which terrorism lurks—extreme poverty; mass unmet needs for jobs, incomes and dignity; and the political and economic instability that results from degrading human conditions.'[13]

In other words, human security in a globalized world depends not just on the absence of war, conflict and terrorism but also on justice, where human needs, as well as political freedoms, are met.

Meanwhile global poverty fuels economic migration—the flood of those from poor countries seeking work in the rich world. In the decade to 2007, two million immigrants entered Britain alone. In his best-selling book *Finding Sanctuary*, Abbot Christopher Jamison writes about 'the comparatively wealthy consumer in the developed world seeking refuge from his own consumerist culture. Yet alongside that there is an equally significant problem of the poor in the developing world also seeking refuge. They seek refuge not from consumerism but from poverty and they do so increasingly by emigrating to the wealthy countries.' The poor, he says, are often 'too busy surviving rather than too busy consuming'[14].

What can be done?

In 2000 the United Nations set, as one of its Millennium Development Goals, the noble aim of halving global poverty by 2015. In 2005, the world's largest ever gathering of political leaders—150 prime ministers and presidents—renewed their commitment to these development goals, as they marked the UN's 60th anniversary in New York.

The bid to make poverty history, as aid agencies describe it, by halving the numbers of people living in absolute poverty—defined as living on less than a dollar a day—is entirely achievable, according to development experts. What is striking is the apparent consensus on this amongst the experts.

An end to global poverty, even by 2025, 'seems like an outlandish claim, an impossible dream,' commented Jeffrey Sacks in his 2007 BBC Reith Lectures. 'But it's within reach. It is a scientifically sound objective. And it is the most urgent challenge of our generation.'

'If there is the will, we really could reduce the number of people living in absolute poverty to under 10 per cent,' commented Peter Rundell, when he was responsible for poverty reduction strategies in the office of the European Commission's Director-General for Development. 'We could save the lives of several hundred million children with relatively small dents in our own pockets. That's the challenge worth rising to. That's what gets me up in the morning,' he told a public forum held in the London centre of Initiatives of Change in May 2005.

Speaking at a similar Greencoat Forum in September 2005, Daleep Mukarji, the Director of the UK aid agency Christian Aid, said, 'We will not win the war on terrorism unless we win the war on poverty.' He noted, in his talk on 'The scandal of poverty: can we make poverty history?', that the world's three richest people were wealthier than the entire population of Africa. The then richest of them all, Microsoft founder Bill Gates, is putting his wealth to good use. The Bill and Melinda Gates Foundation, with an endowment of some $33 billion, is the largest transparently operated foundation in the world. It tackles health care issues, such as HIV/Aids, and extreme poverty, and is larger than most country donors.

Jeffrey Sacks gives it a further 10 years beyond the 2015 target set by the Millennium Development Goals, to 2025, to eliminate extreme poverty. 'The wealth of the rich world, the power of today's vast storehouses of knowledge, and the declining fractions of the world that needs help to escape from poverty all make the end of poverty a realistic possibility by the year 2025.'[15]

Good and bad trends

Already the proportion of the world's population living in absolute poverty has declined from 40 per cent in 1981 to 21 per cent in 2005. In numbers this meant a reduction from 1.5 billion to 1.1 billion people. In 2007 the UN reported that the figure had fallen to just under a billion. In South Asia, in the two decades between 1981 and 2001, the percentage was reduced from just over 50 per cent to just over 30 per cent, while the fall in East Asia was far more dramatic: from nearly 60 per cent to around 15 per cent. The World Bank forecasts that those living on only a dollar a day will fall to 10.2 per cent of the world's population by 2015. In Sub-Saharan Africa the trend, till recently, was in the wrong direction. There the proportion of those living in extreme poverty rose during those two decades from just over 40 per cent to 45 per cent.[16] Between 2000 and 2004 the figure fell back to 41 per cent but this was still twice the global percentage.

'The headline figure of 200 million lifted out of extreme poverty... during the 1990s provides a misleading impression of serene progress,' comments Edward Bickham, a senior executive at Anglo American mining corporation. 'The truth is that 150 million of these people are in China—whilst some of sub-Saharan Africa actually went backwards.' His company, a big investor in Africa and Latin America, employs some 200,000 people, of which 120,000 are in sub-Saharan Africa[17]. The company is committed to treating its South African employees who suffer from HIV/AIDS, nearly a quarter of whom are affected. For his part, Anglo American's Chairman, Sir Mark Moody-Stuart, is a leading advocate of sustainable development, as a member of the UN's Global Compact for socially responsible business. He urges 'all sections of society', including big business, to play their part[18]. A signatory to a Tomorrow's Global Company report, he calls for businesses to 'play a greater role in contributing to solving the problems that society faces, including environmental degradation, poverty and the abuse of human rights'[19].

Jeffrey Sacks commented, in his Reith Lectures, that 'Africa has not so much been harmed by globalization, as bypassed by it. The basic challenge is to help Africa and other still impoverished regions onto the development ladder.' The development challenges facing African countries were food production, disease, 'miserably deficient infrastructure' and 'the continuing surge of population'. Yet there are also major investment opportunities in Africa. Ghana's stock market, for instance, has surprisingly been one of the best performing in the world. Over the whole continent, growth has averaged over five per cent in recent years, driven in part by China's and India's demand for primary commodities.

Gordon Brown, when Britain's Chancellor of the Exchequer, led the charge in urging rich countries to meet the UN's target of giving 0.7 per cent of their GNP in development aid—another of the Millennium Development Goals. Aid, fair trade that allows access to Western markets, debt remission and the war against corruption, waged by Transparency International and others, all play a vital role in poverty reduction.

Corruption exacerbates poverty, due to the misappropriation of resources. 'Corruption is to take and use; integrity means sharing and giving,' commented Lord Daniel Brennan, a Labour life peer and lawyer, at the opening of the conference 'Globalizing integrity; personalizing integrity', held at the Initiatives of Change centre in Caux, Switzerland, in 2006. He stressed the importance of promoting responsible capitalism on a foundation of integrity and realism.

The Caux Round Table group of senior business executives, which he chairs, seeks to promote integrity and fight corruption. According to Lord Brennan, some $50 billion went in aid to poorer countries, at a time when $500 billion in dirty money went the other way.

Few suggest that aid should be withheld because of such high levels of corruption, as this would merely punish the poor who should benefit the most from aid flows. Some argue that increasing aid perpetuates a dependency culture, but Sacks points out that food production, disease control and infrastructure 'require public-sector investments beyond the levels that impoverished African countries can afford'. Meanwhile, too many of the political elites have benefitted from grand scale corruption, undermining the people's trust in their governance.

For instance, a corrupt collusion between politicians and local mafia bosses perpetuates the slums of Mumbai and Calcutta, says Sarosh Ghandy, a former senior executive of the Tata industrial group and now Director of the Centre for Training in Ethical Leadership (CENTREL) in Bangalore. 'When the government puts up low cost housing to give the slum dwellers alternative accommodation, does it result in the slum dwelling being torn down? No. The mafia don arranges for someone else to occupy the dwelling. The slums are supplied electricity through illegal tapping and water is similarly stolen.' Ghandy sites this as a crass example of poor governance.

An historic chance

Yet there are many examples of good governance and wealth creation, especially in the private sector, as the next chapters show.

Businesses and enterprises can exploit or they can contribute towards sustainable development. The global private sector 'has a capacity and an ability to invest and to participate in the development effort which wasn't possible 20 years ago,' said Turkish-born Kemal Dervis in his first speech as the new Administrator of the United Nations Development Programme (UNDP).[20] This was one reason, he asserted, that 'we may really be at a historic moment, where the fight against poverty and associated ills, such as disease, really enters a new critical phase. We may be able to achieve an amount of progress that was not possible in the past.' The engine of private growth in the developing countries, says Sir Jim Lester, for many years Chairman of the UK's annual Worldaware Awards for developing-world entrepreneurs, contributes to 'a safer, more prosperous, more equal world'.

If this is the case, what, then, are the motivations of the entre-preneurs who are the world's wealth creators? How do they see their role in poverty reduction? What qualities of integrity and leadership do they show? And how does the world develop a 'moral capitalism' in the phrase of Stephen Young, Global Executive Director of the Caux Round Table group of business leaders? There is a clear link between enterprise and poverty reduction, for it is business people and entrepreneurs who create jobs, skills and wealth. 'If we want less poverty, then of necessity we must have more business,' comments Young. 'Not everyone of course is happy with this. It brings into relief the long term limitations of mere charity and the responsibilities of local elites to be honest and just with their national patrimonies.'

Motivation is one of the key factors in human performance. Yet the need to understand motivation, beyond the imperatives of the bottom line and shareholder value, seems to be under-rated. Adam Smith, the father of modern capitalism, wrote *The Wealth of Nations*. But he also penned *The Theory of Moral Sentiments*. Stephen Young argues that the separation of these two texts has given the world a distorted notion of how the cap-italist and enterprise system should work. 'Smith's two books are part of one vision,' Young told the opening of the Caux Conference for Business and Industry, Switzerland, in 2001. 'The human person [Smith maintained] needs the dimension of right and wrong: you cannot be truly human without having a moral sense.' As Germany's literary giant, Goethe, said, 'Treat others as if they are what they should be and they will become what they should be.'

This emphasis on 'human development' is the critical factor in economic development, says Sarosh Ghandy of CENTREL. 'The highest priority has to be given to ways of improving gover-nance and putting human development on the fast track. Unless we take this by the horns we will keep throwing money into a bottomless pit,' he says. Human development indices usually focus on the investment in human capital—health, education and life expectancy. But Ghandy describes human development as the will to 'develop oneself as a better person. Too many of us

23

are filled with too much pride. We allow our pride and ego to influence our decision-making, with disastrous results. A good person is a humble person who wants to spread joy and happiness around him.' For Ghandy, then, human development is concerned with growth in character and conscience. Indeed, capitalism without conscience leads to corruption.

Peter Rundell, now a senior official at the UK's Department for International Development, comments that 'our focus on maximizing what we can measure, and our predilection for more money, have led to the glorification of GDP. Perhaps progress with measurement of happiness may point up the predictive power of developing better people, not simply strong or more educated people.' He quotes the great Jewish theologian Rabbi Abraham Heschel who remarked, 'When I was young I respected people who were clever. Now I'm older I respect people who are kind.'

I have been struck, over the years in which I have written articles for the British press, by the stories of those engaged in business and enterprise, agriculture and development, and sometimes a combination of all these, who have shown a profound moral, ethical and, indeed, spiritual motivation and purpose in life, including concern for poverty reduction and environmental sustainability. They have a wider sense of their stakeholders than the traditional business ones of employees, customers, shareholders, suppliers and local community. They have included notions of nationhood, the global community, justice, and the legacy to future generations, as part of their mandate. None of them would claim to be saints. But they have pursued their role in life, through ups and downs, victories and setbacks, with a sense of calling and vision over the long haul. They have walked the talk. They are making a world of difference.

1. Al Gore, *An Inconvenient Truth*, introduction, 2006
2. 'Clearing a path out of poverty' by Timothy Garton Ash, *The Independent*, 31 January 2001
3. See www.ipcc.ch
4. *BBC One TV news*, 5 July 2006

5. David Smith, *The Dragon and the Elephant: China, India and the New World Order*, Profile Books, 2007, page 238

6. Quoted by Edward Luce in his book, *In spite of the Gods: the strange rise of modern India*, Little, Brown, 2006, page 280

7. Mike Davis, *Planet of Slums*, Verso, 2006

8. *Newsweek* magazine, 'The New India', 6 March 2006

9. Joseph Stiglitz, *Globalization and its discontents*, 2002, and *Making globalization work*, 2006

10. For the up-to-date position on debt cancellation see www.jubileedebtcampaign.org.uk

11. Addressing the 32nd annual Caux Conference for Business and Industry, Caux, Switzerland, July 2004

12. Speaking in Sierra Leone, on his first visit to Africa, Tony Blair described African poverty as 'a scar on the conscience of humanity', February 2002

13. Jeffrey Sacks, *The End of Poverty*, Penguin Books, 2005, page 215

14. Christopher Jamison, *Finding Sanctuary*, Weidenfeld & Nicolson, 2006, page 133

15. Sacks, page 5

16. Ibid, page 22

17. Edward Bickham, executive vice-president: external affairs, Anglo American plc, writing in the company's magazine, *Optima*, February 2005

18. *For A Change* magazine, December 2003

19. Published by the business think-tank Tomorrow's Company, June 2007

20. 16 August 2005

2

Tatas redefine the bottom line

*India's leading industrial empire is producing
social capital as well as profits.*

As you drive along a dusty road, past parched fields east of the
steel city of Jamshedpur, a large brick college building comes
into view. It dominates the tribal hamlet of Asanboni. The college serves 500 students from some 75 villages, in one of the
poorest regions of eastern India. It was opened in 1993 by
Jamshed Irani, then Managing Director of the huge Tata Iron
and Steel Company (Tisco) in Jamshedpur. A local *adivasi* (tribal)
leader, Shailendra Mahato, had persuaded the company to fund
the building's construction, as part of its social welfare policy.

The Tata Group—India's largest private sector conglomerate,
comprising 91 companies employing some 220,000 people—is
renowned worldwide for its commitment to social development. Western businesses may have discovered the virtues of
'corporate social responsibility', but Tata has been practising it
for decades in a nation that has virtually no welfare safety net.
Housing for employees, company-run hospitals and schools,
and rural development projects such as road building, tree
planting and well digging, are all part of the Tata approach. Tata
Steel introduced the world's first eight-hour working day, back
in 1912, and today employees are deemed to be at work from
the moment they leave their homes and are paid accordingly.
The Tata companies are majority owned (66 per cent) by 10 Tata
philanthropic trusts, which benefit from company profits,

rather than just the shareholders or Tata family members.

Revolutionary indeed. But not all has been plain sailing. In January 2006 there were violent clashes between tribal villagers and police at Kalinganagar, an area rich in iron ore reserves in the state of Orissa. The district administration has allocated a 2,000-acre site there for Tata to build a new steel plant, which will be the third largest in India. But when the company started erecting a boundary wall, tribal leaders led protests saying they had not been adequately compensated for the land. Police opened fire and 21 people were killed. Now the company is negotiating directly with landowners to ensure a fair price.

In recent years Tata's social ethos has also been under threat, due to globalization. Just at the time when Asanboni's village college was opened, India was also opening its doors to global competition through trade liberalization and reduction of import tariffs. This put enormous pressure on companies to cut costs. Tisco, for instance, has claimed to produce the cheapest steel in the world, but it achieved this by cutting jobs dramatically, from 85,000 people in 1991 to 44,000 in 2005[1].

Some feared that the Tata group would find it increasingly tough to maintain its social welfare commitments. With an expanding domestic and global market, however, the Tata Group has seen dramatic increases in its earnings. Revenues were $17.6 billion in 2004-05, the equivalent of nearly three per cent of India's GDP, and over twice its revenues of five years before. In 2005 they were even higher at $24 billion.[2] Then in 2006 Tata Steel made a successful bid to take over the Anglo-Dutch steel company Corus, beating off competition from Brazil.

The biggest challenge facing the Tata empire is 'how to be an international company and, at the same time, maintain its soul,' said R Gopalakrishnan, Executive Director of Tata Sons, Tata's parent company, when I met him in the Tata headquarters in downtown Mumbai in 2003. In his view the company's soul lay in its social involvement.

Anant Nadkarni, who oversees Tata's community initiatives, says the way to maintain Tata's social ethos is through 'a holistic approach'. Tata may have to 'look beyond its current social expenditure', he says. This was $86 million in 2005-2006. But throwing money at development 'misses the point. It is not a question of cheque book philanthropy but of personal involvement. We need to innovate. It is like a river confronted by a mountain. The river has to go round.'

Michael Smith

Anant Nadkarni

So how has Tata innovated? By getting its employees to volunteer for community service. 'Tata companies now treat corporate social responsibility more strategically, using technology to improve peoples' quality of life, especially for the poor,' says Nadkarni, who is Vice-President, Group Corporate Social Responsibility. 'We have 11,500 registered volunteers who clock on an average of over one million volunteering hours annually.' Employees typically give 3-4 hours each week.

Nadkarni sees this as being holistic 'because it is very therapeutic'. Serving the less fortunate in the villages 'is a way of understanding yourself', he says. 'Modern systems of management,' he believes, 'are not designed to release the true potential of individuals whilst achieving the company's ends. But community service does that.' He quotes Sir Edmund Hillary: 'It is not the mountain we have to conquer but ourselves.'

Nadkarni talks about the 'push and pull' influences on his own 27-year career in Tata, which have led to his current position. He received higher education, housing and medical care at Tata Engineering in Pune where he was an internal auditor. 'Tata gives promotions and rewards without leaving a sense of obligation for the receiver,' he says. 'This gradually transforms you into being a giver yourself.' When he was bored by mundane work on production targets, he volunteered to mentor two non-governmental organizations in Pune. He built up some 25 citizens' groups under the National Society for Clean Cities, in liaison with the municipal authority, and became joint coordinator of the Express Citizens' Forum. This community work gave him an opportunity, he says, for 'self-expression, problem solving and creativity'.

Two friends stood by him at that time. They were connected with Asia Plateau, the Initiatives of Change centre in Panchgani, a hill resort in the mountains south of Pune, where they invited Nadkarni in 1992. 'This reinforced a lot of what I had earlier believed, but the process there took me further in realizing that change begins with me.' This encouraged Nadkarni to make his long-term career shift within Tata, three years later, to pioneer the Tata Council for Community Initiatives (TCCI) as its first operating head.

In 2004 he spoke about Tata's social commitments at a business and industry conference in Caux, Switzerland. The visit also had an unexpected personal effect: a friend there helped him to quit smoking—urging him not to die a slow death through smoking 'the weed'.

Nadkarni points to the many initiatives that have emerged through TCCI. A designer at Tata Automation developed a new type of artificial limb, which could be adopted globally. An officer from Tata Engineering in Jamshedpur set up a care centre that rehabilitates people cured of leprosy. And Tata Consultancy Services, Asia's largest software firm, developed an adult literacy education system that claims to teach 60-year-olds to read a newspaper within three weeks. 'This initiative is greatly impacting the pace at which the nation's Adult Literacy Programme is being implemented,' Nadkarni believes.

Tata's enlightened approach could become part of a wider trend. In 2004, Tata Industries was one of the 30 international companies to submit 'triple bottom line' accounting, measuring not just their financial results but also their social and environmental practice, to the United Nations Global Reporting Initiative.

Tata has also developed its index for sustainable human development, measuring 'human excellence', similar to the Human Development Index of the United Nations

Development Programme. 'This is the first time that any corporation in the world has applied the Human Development Index principles through a business process,' Nadkarni says. Tata remains the only corporation to have worked with the UNDP on this and Nadkarni claims this has had 'an outstanding impact on improving the quality of life' of employees.

The company has also sought the help of the Confederation of Indian Industries in creating a network of companies that maintain community initiatives.

Nadkarni says that there has never been any resistance to Tata's social expenditure from its two million shareholders. Nor, he claims, do Tata executives see community involvement as a means of burnishing the company's reputation. They have even been known to remove 'sponsored by Tata' signs from village initiatives, he says.

So what's in it for Tata? 'I don't see the need for the question at all,' Nadkarni replies briskly. 'Gautam Buddha left his house to seek enlightenment over three questions: how to deal with disease, old age and death. But when enlightenment did happen, in that paradigm shift he almost forgot the initial questions. So, if you ask, "What is the business sense in this?" you are not the man I may want to work with.' He agrees with R M Lala, author of a best-selling book on the house of Tata, *The Creation of Wealth*, who says that wealth is far more than profit or income generation. It is to do with 'weal, which means well-being or happiness' of the communities that businesses serve. And that, says Nadkarni, is what Tata is determined to maintain.

Updated from articles first published in Guardian Weekly, 10-16 April 2003, headlined 'Indian industrial empire redefines bottom line'; For A Change magazine June/July 2003; and the Tata Review 2004.

1. Edward Luce, *In spite of the Gods: the strange rise of modern India*, 2006, page 51
2. *Newsweek* cover story, *The New India*, 6 March 2006

3

No bribes for healthy business

Corruption is bad for business and bad for health, says Suresh Vazirani, Managing Director of an award-winning hi-tech company.

IT MUST have been in Suresh Vazirani's *karma* to develop life-saving medical technology, says his wife, Mala. For in his heart he had wanted to be a doctor. Instead, his parents sent him, one of seven children, on a scholarship to study electrical engineering at Nagpur University in central India. This turned out to be fortuitous, for his engineering training has stood him in good stead. Vazirani now runs a multi award-winning medical technology company, manufacturing state-of-the-art blood biochemistry analysers.

Imagine the scenario: you are in hospital for a routine operation or perhaps with a life-threatening illness—malaria, say, or TB or hepatitis or even HIV/Aids. The doctors need to diagnose exactly what you've got. And they need to know fast. They take a sample of your blood and run it through a blood analyser. Vazirani's machines can do up to 600 tests in an hour, for over 200 blood diseases. They save lives.

His company, Transasia Biomedicals, based in Mumbai, is India's market leader in manufacturing such high-tech blood diagnostic machines. The best hospitals in India, making use of these machines, have an international reputation, thanks to the skills of their highly trained medical staff and the technology available. Increasingly, Western patients make the journey to India for private life-saving operations at a fraction of the cost back home. 'Medical tourism' to India is booming. It is set to

Blair Cummock

Suresh Vazirani

reach $2.3 billion a year by 2012, according to the Confederation of Indian Industry.[1]

Vazirani, the chief executive, laid Transasia's foundations in 1985, initially as an importing company. Today Transasia is a global player with exports to some 50 countries.

'Helping people leads to market leadership' headlined *The Japan Times* over an article about Vazirani's company in 2004. 'The urge to help others, rather than a pure profit motive, lies behind the genesis of one medical technology company that has risen to the top of its niche market,' the paper wrote[2].

In 2005, the company won both the Government of India's National Research and Development Award and India's first ever Emerging India Award as 'the most promising small and medium sized enterprise' of the year, out of 5,000 entrants. Receiving the award, Vazirani commented that 'business and industry should provide the healing touch and play their part to create a better world for all.' Earlier, in 2000, Transasia won first prize in India's National Exports Awards for advanced technology, presented to Vazirani by the then Prime Minister, Atal Bihari Vajpayee. The Prime Minister also presented Vazirani's wife, Mala, with the National Quality Award for the leading biotechnology company.

Even more than the prizes, what especially marks out the Vaziranis is their courageous and dogged stance against corruption. Avoiding corruption takes up more of his time than any other issue, Vazirani says. His company employs two lawyers full-time to fight the cases that arise. When, for instance, he wanted to install a fountain in the lunch area, two government officials demanded a $100 bribe for a licence. Yet no such licences had been issued for 20 years. It took his lawyers four years in the courts, costing $4,000, to deal with the case. But Vazirani feels it is worth making a stand on such issues, as his company's reputation for integrity is paramount.

His parents had fled from Pakistan at the time of Partition in 1947, bringing nothing with them. As a young man, Vazirani had blamed the politicians for his family's deprivation and for corruption. Therefore, he says, he regarded it as his right to travel without paying for a ticket and to

Transasia won first prize in India's National Exports Awards for advanced technology in 2000.

steal library books. But then he encountered Moral Re-Armament (now Initiatives of Change) and this challenged him 'to walk the talk, to rise above blame towards responsibility'.

On graduation, he decided to be an unpaid volunteer with MRA, helping to run industrial leadership training programmes at Asia Plateau, MRA's conference centre near Pune. There he would urge businessmen not to be corrupt, he recalls. That's all very well, they would reply, but you've never run a business. You don't know what it's like.

The challenge rankled with Vazirani, but he knew it had some truth. So when after nine years with MRA he needed to earn an income, he decided to go into business himself. In 1979 he and a friend, Satish Sutaria, registered the company name of Transasia, 'as a reminder of Asia Plateau', Vazirani says. He was 29 and had just 250 rupees (about £4) to his name.

Their idea was to create an importing and marketing company. They had no capital to start a factory, and not even enough to rent an office. But thanks to their experience with MRA, says Mala, 'they wanted to do something of central relevance, definitely in industry, health care or social services. They wanted to make a difference where it really could count.' Sutaria's mother sold some jewellery to help them get started, and a dental manufacturing businessman, Surendra Patel, and his wife, Dhara, let them use their dining room in the Mumbai suburb of Andheri as an office. From there they wrote 100 letters to companies all over the world, offering their marketing services, but with hardly any response.

Then Dhara's brother sold an apartment and offered to loan the money to Vazirani. Sutaria felt uneasy about whether they could ever repay the loan. But Vazirani leapt at the opportunity and, taking the biggest gamble of his life, bought a six-month round-the-world air ticket. He wanted to find out what the world was making that India most needed. This was too much for Sutaria, who decided to quit the partnership.

Vazirani visited medical manufacturing companies in Florence and Rome—it was unprecedented for an Indian marketer to turn up on the doorstep. In Tokyo he met a dynamic young export manager, Shimoyama, also handling medical machines, who had visited India after his graduation. They immediately established a rapport and Shimoyama felt he could trust Vazirani to give good customer service. These encounters gave Vazirani his big break and he returned to Mumbai a fully signed up distributor of Italian and Japanese medical diagnostic machines.

He knew little about the machine parts or their application but he set to, clearing the imported machines through customs, installing them and training the customers.

But it was a big leap from importing to manufacturing. The potential market was vast, not only in India but also in China and Africa. The imported machines were expensive and prone to failure. The service engineers that Vazirani employed gave him the confidence that they could assemble them locally themselves.

A critical moment came in 1991 when Vazirani was badly let down by one of the Italian firms. He had the orders from customers, but the machines never arrived. Exasperated, he flew to

Rome and visited the company every day for 15 days before concluding that they were never going to deliver. 'That experience in Rome really crystallized things for me—that if we were to come up to customers' expectations, and if I was to control my own destiny, we had to start manufacturing ourselves. It was a question of our credibility.'

Back in Andheri his staff of 25 was so enthusiastic that they built their first prototype within two months. 'We said to each other, "Wow, we can do it. Why didn't we do it all along?"' That first model had 70 per cent imported parts. From then on they developed a new model each year and now, in a classic case of what economists call import substitution, the foreign content is less than 25 per cent. 'We were able to give tough competition to the bigger American, German and Japanese companies,' Vazirani says.

The company faced tougher competition when, between 1995 and 1997, the government cut import tariffs from 40 per cent to five per cent, under World Trade Organization rules. 'We had to see globalization as an opportunity rather than a threat,' Vazirani says. He calculated that, while the company manufactured 5,000 machines a year for the domestic market, they could produce 20,000 for the world market, provided they could make a machine with a really big capacity.

In 1996, he revisited Japan at a time when the yen was rising, making the large Japanese machines prohibitively expensive abroad. Over three days he negotiated an agreement with a Japanese company that would give him the technology to manufacture the machines in India, in return for a royalty for each one that Transasia sold. 'It was a win-win situation,' Vazirani says. 'Here was a Japanese company willing to give us the technology with not much down payment purely on the basis of trust.' This first venture into the top end of the market was a dream fulfilled for Vazirani. When a supercilious German distributor visited Transasia, 'You should have seen his face,' Vazirani says. 'His mouth was open. He couldn't believe his eyes. We started supplying to him and it was a very good contract.'

Along with the exports came the fight against corruption. Vazirani risked losing a DM20 million sales contract to Germany because a customs officer wanted a bribe to release vital imported components. Rather than paying up, Vazirani left the components in the warehouse for three months. He went to the top customs officials, arguing that if Transasia didn't get this order the country would lose. 'We appealed to their sense of national pride.' The components were released just in time for Transasia to win the contract.

Recently, a politician suggested to Vazirani that it would be 'an opportunity' if they each pocketed part of the World Bank aid the politician had received to improve health care. 'Yes, and is it an opportunity if we land up in hospital needing urgent care ourselves?' replied Vazirani. At this, the politician realized that Vazirani was not to be bought and hastily changed his tune. He even promised to increase state aid to hospitals.

In September 2003, Vazirani was a keynote speaker at the launch in Mumbai of Transparency International's new Business Principles for Combating Bribery. 'Corruption is a big road block to progress,' he says. 'Because of it everything goes wrong. The intimidation leads to wrong decision-making. Transasia can be an example. But many more companies need to be.'

He now has a vision to found an Indian institute of leadership, which would provide a two-year post-graduate training programme for around 100 young people who wish to enter public life. The trainees, drawn from all over India, would need to commit themselves to ethical values. The programme would have its own residential and teaching/reseach building at the Asia Plateau campus in Panchgani. Vazirani is providing the initial capital cost of US$500,000.

In all he does, Vazirani is wholeheartedly supported by his effervescent wife, Mala. They were introduced by their parents and 'we took off'—an ideal match–'much to everyone's surprise, including ourselves,' Mala says. They now have three children. It was her idea to supply 35 blood analysers at a special low price to small clinics for the benefit of slum dwellers.

Today Transasia, with an annual turn-over of around US$30 million, employs 600 people in three locations, one near the airport, and two 150 kilometres up the coast in the state of Gujarat. The company's research and development department has over 50 scientists, software engineers and bio-medical professionals[3].

'It has been a wonderful, and at times tough, learning experience,' comments Vazirani. 'But I know it is part of God's plan. So I never get worried about the problems. God gives the power and I am sure he gives the solutions too. Whenever I come to a junction, I find someone taking my hand and making sure I take the right turn.'

www.transasia.co.in

Updated from an article first published in For A Change *magazine, December 2003.*
See also Vazirani's story in Global Corruption Report 2006, on 'Corruption and Health', page 58, published by Transparency International and Pluto Press.

1. *The Daily Telegraph*, London, 11 February 2006.

2. *The Japan Times*, 20 November 2004.

3. Ibid.

4

Rubber Soul

*Mumbai businessman Rajendra Gandhi has made recycling
a matter of moral principle.*

LIKE MANY in India, Rajendra Gandhi looks forward to the day
when India might stage Formula 1 motor racing. He has a special interest, for his company would be in the market to recycle
the worn tyres.

'Creating wealth out of waste', as he puts it, appeals to
Gandhi, Managing Director of Gujurat Reclaim and Rubber
Products Ltd (GRRP). What better product to do so than
rubber? It is non-biodegradable, so recycling it is environmentally friendly. Old tyres and tubes—from buses and bicycles,
cars and coaches, tractors and trucks—as well as used latex
gloves and worn hose pipes all pass through the company's two
plants in the states of Gujurat and Maharashtra.

GRRP is India's largest rubber recycling company and is
among the top four in the world. It supplies the world's major
tyre companies: Bridgestone Firestone, Continental Tyres,
Cooper, Dunlop and Pirelli.

But what also appeals to Gandhi is running a company without the compromises of corruption. He founded GRRP in 1973
after reading a World Bank report which said that recycling
would be an up-and-coming business in developing countries.
'I was quite fired up by that thought,' he says. But in those days

Prime Minister Indira Gandhi ran a much more centrally-controlled economy than today's liberalized one. That might have meant having to pay bribes, says Gandhi.

GRRP

Rajendra Gandhi

'If I had gone into any other industry I would have come under a quota system in the controlled economy,' he explains. 'I would have needed a quota license for getting raw materials, and it was customary to bribe government officials to get the maximum quota. But my raw material was scrap rubber and I didn't need to bribe anyone to get that as it was readily available.' A liberalized economy, he implies, is a potentially less corrupt one. He relies on a network of agents who supply the scrap rubber from all over India.

Gandhi also pioneered the design and manufacture of machinery for rubber recycling in India. Again, his motive was to avoid the corruption involved in importing technology from overseas. 'To get an import license you had to pay bribes to officials in New Delhi.' So Gandhi asked a rubber technologist, WG Desai, if it was possible to make the machinery himself. Desai said it was. 'It was a big risk for me as I had no knowledge of the industry,' says Gandhi. 'But with his help and with the support of bank loans we started to put the technology together.'

He needed seven million rupees ($US250,000 in those days) in start-up capital, which came from bank and family loans as well as a public issue of shares. The company's launch was delayed when Prime Minister Indira Gandhi declared a State of Emergency in 1975, which included restrictions on paying dividends. Rajendra Gandhi's plan to raise the capital through a public issue collapsed. He finally raised the money needed in 1977, after the Emergency ended, and went into production in 1978.

The process involves pulverizing the old rubber into powder and sifting out any metal and fabric. The powder is treated with oils and chemicals under heat and the resultant soft rubber is made into flat sheets, cut to size according to the customers' packaging requirements, and sold by the ton. The company processes some 27,000 tons of reclaimed rubber per year, out of India's total of 80,000 tons.

None of this might have happened had Gandhi not overcome his fear of his father, a process of which he speaks frankly and openly. Vadilal Gandhi was the owner of Ashok Silk Mills, in the Mumbai suburb of Ghatkopar, and a local Congress politician. He had a reputation for philanthropy but at home had a fiery temper. He sent his son off to boarding school at the age of nine and from there Rajendra went to live in a student hostel at Mumbai's prestigious Indian Institute of Technology (IIT), where he studied metallurgy. His father remained a remote figure.

Travelling on a bus one day, the young Gandhi found himself sitting next to a Westerner who was reading a copy of a magazine called *Himmat*. 'The fact that he was travelling on a bus amused me,' says Gandhi, as whites usually went by taxi. He engaged him in conversation. The man, from Wales, was working on the staff of the magazine in India. He invited Gandhi to see a film which was going to be shown in a downtown apartment on Marine Drive.

Rajendra thought that it would be a Hollywood movie. But it turned out to be very different from what he expected: a drama dealing with racial conflict in colonial Africa. A young Indian at the film show invited Gandhi to the opening of a new residential block at the MRA centre in the hill town of Panchgani. The centre, a day's drive from Mumbai, was being built by Rajmohan Gandhi, a grandson of Mahatma Gandhi, who at that time was the Editor-in-Chief of *Himmat*.

'There I was challenged to look at my life,' says Rajendra Gandhi. 'I had the clear thought to share my life with my parents. I was very afraid of my father. So I wrote a letter to him in a tone of honesty and apology.' Rajendra had been spending his monthly pocket money on movies and 'vulgar' books whilst telling his parents that it was going on text books. He wrote in the letter to his father: 'This is the type of son you've had and I have decided to change my life.' He gave the letter to his mother to give to his father, 'because I didn't have the courage to give it to him', he recalls.

When his father read it he summoned his son from the hostel to his room at their home. For five minutes his father didn't say a word. Then he said, 'I feel very sad that you have been up to all this mischief.' He gave his son a piece of his mind, but Rajendra noticed that he didn't flair up into a temper. Then, to his surprise, his father began to talk about the things he had got up to his own childhood. 'As he talked I could feel the generation gap, that wall from him, breaking. And I felt a respect for him, coming out of love instead of fear.'

Not long afterwards Rajendra borrowed his father's new transistor radio, when he was away on business and without his permission, to listen to a cricket commentary. Within a day it was stolen from his room at the IIT. He was overcome by fear of facing his father again. 'In a time of quiet reflection I knew I must own up by going to him straight away. When he returned two or three days later I told him and said I was sorry. He really raised hell and said I was an irresponsible young man. I knew I had to take this with humility and face the consequences.'

The surprising effect of all this on Rajendra was to remove the fear he had of his father. He found it gave him the courage to discuss and disagree with him on business matters.

Rajendra Gandhi graduated in metallurgy in 1971, and at first joined his father's silk mill. But after reading a World Bank report on recycling, he asked his father's permission to start his own business.

'He really supported me,' says Rajendra. 'I didn't want to live in the legacy of what my father was doing. My decision to be honest with him gave me the courage to approach him; otherwise I might have remained under his shadow and control. Instead he allowed me to use family money to start my own business.'

GRRP made a profit of US$2.4 million after tax in 2006-07, on a turnover of $21 million—up by $8 million on the previous year—and the company now exports to 35 countries.

But what most satisfies Gandhi is to know that his plants, in Ankleshar, Gujurat, and Sholapur, Maharashtra, have given jobs to 500 people 'at well above the minimum wage'.

First published in For A Change magazine, December 2005.

5

In the aftermath of tragedy

Sri Lankan editor and bookseller Vijitha Yapa lost relatives in the Asian tsunami. Now he and his family are involved in reconstruction.

It was only three days before the Asian tsunami struck on Boxing Day 2004 that Sri Lankan bookseller Vijitha Yapa decided to give the day off to his staff of eight at his bookshop, situated a few yards from the southern coast in Galle. For the previous 10 years they had all worked on Boxing Day. But this year the day coincided with the Buddhist holiday of Poya.

His decision saved their lives. The bookshop, 50 metres from the beach, was flooded to the ceiling before the water burst through the front door carrying the books on to the street. Yapa lost about US$200,000 worth of stock. 'The schools were due to restart in January, the tourist hotels in the south were full and that is why we had so much stock.'

A few doors away, three of his cousins were killed in their restaurant which was reduced to rubble. Their bodies were never found. His 84-year-old uncle was also killed. He lived half a mile inland and died from the fright of seeing the waves bringing in a 40-foot boat which smashed through the boundary wall of his house. His daughter held onto his hand but could not save him. It was the next day before the undertakers could reach the house.

What shocked Yapa as much as anything was to hear that a man was found still alive, buried under the rubble just outside his shop, a week after the disaster.

The insurance companies 'suddenly become very religious', initially refusing to cover losses because the tsunami was called an act of God. 'You can quote religion but don't forget that God also gave you a conscience and we insure for emergencies,' Yapa told his insurers. They finally gave him only a small per cent of the stock value and he faced a trading loss for the year.

Yapa was moved by the sight of children hanging out their soaked text books to dry in the sun. Within one month of the tsunami, and without waiting for insurance, he reopened his shop—the first on Galle's Main Street to reopen amidst the rubble-filled streets. Instead of a door, there were planks. Instead of racks, there were makeshift tables. He was determined to have at least the school supplies available for the children. 'We didn't want to deprive the children of what they needed: exercise books, pens, stationery and text books. One of our first customers was an Italian who wanted to give 80,000 rupees worth of books to donate to the local schools.'

Yapa tells about the principal of one school in Galle who had called a meeting to discuss timetables on the day the disaster struck. One of the teachers present, who was pregnant, saw the wave coming and climbed onto the table. As the wave crashed through the door, the principal and the pregnant woman were holding hands but were pulled apart. The woman held on to a wooden plank from the table, but they never found the body of the principal.

Some children lost both their parents and stared out at the sea, waiting for them to return. A salesman told Yapa, 'We lived beside the sea, our friend. Can we ever trust it now?'

Two months after the tsunami, Yapa was re-elected President of Sri Lanka's Booksellers Association, a position he had previously held for two years. His family business owns the largest chain of English-language bookshops in Sri Lanka. He is also the nation's largest English-language publisher. The 12 bookshops, employing 150 people, generate an annual turn-over of US$2 million. He imports more books from Britain than anyone else, air-freighting in one ton each week. At any one time he has a quarter of a million titles in stock.

Despite his losses, Yapa used his position to campaign to give free books to the 200 schools whose libraries were destroyed by the tsunami. 'What is my loss compared to the suffering of these children?' he asked. The Booksellers Association made an initial donation of 100,000 rupees to cover the costs of transporting and warehousing new text books. A British man in Oxford, who was born on a tea plantation in Sri Lanka, raised £700 towards the fund. Time Warner was the only international publishing house to donate books.

At a ceremony in February 2006, in the auditorium of the Ministry of Education, Yapa handed over a consignment of books to the principals of the tsunami-damaged schools, including Navodya (New Beginning) English-language schools. The ceremony was organized by the Ministry of Education and books were provided by booksellers, publishers and donors. One head teacher told the ministry officials: 'You are giving our children English books. But what do we do without English teachers?' Some of them had also been killed in the tsunami. Over a year later Sri Lanka was still coming to terms with its terrible losses.

Vijitha Yapa came to book selling following his earlier career in journalism. His training was on the English-language newsweekly *Himmat* in Mumbai, India, published by a grandson of Mahatma Gandhi. Yapa worked there for three years, from 1972 to 1975, and his time there also revealed his flair for sales and marketing. When his visa expired he returned to Sri Lanka, became the Media Manager for the Board of Investment, and then gave this up to represent *The Asian Wall Street Journal* published by Dow Jones. He and his wife Lalana started Vijitha Yapa Associates in April 1981 and today they import and distribute the world's best known newspapers and magazines including the *Wall Street Journal, International Herald Tribune, Newsweek, The Economist* and *Reader's Digest*.

In August 1981 the millionaire business tycoon Upali Wijewardene invited Yapa to be the founding editor of his new daily paper *The Island* and offered Yapa the highest ever salary and perks given to an editor in Sri Lanka. Yapa agreed on one condition: 'No interference in the independent newspaper I will create'. Wijewardene kept to his word, even when front page stories reflected badly on his family. 'I did not make you editor to change things according to the whims and fancies or friendships of my family or me,' he once reminded Yapa, when he as editor was asked by a family member to bury a critical article on the inside pages.

But when Wijewardene was killed in an air crash the new management treated Yapa's editorial independence with suspicion. A Sinhala journalist was promoted over him whilst he was abroad, indicating a change in editorial policy. Yapa immediately resigned, with the full support of his wife, Lalana. 'It is better for people to remember you for your independent views than as one who stuck on to the job and sacrificed your principles because the pay was good,' she told him. It was she who ran the family business while Yapa was busy with *The Island* newspaper.

Six months later, he was asked to revive the then defunct Sri Lankan *Sunday Times*, as its new editor. Within 18 months, it had captured the second largest Sunday circulation. *The Times* of London appointed him as their correspondent in Sri Lanka.

But it was not in journalism that Yapa gained one of his most important managerial lessons in life, he says. Surprisingly it was when he was working for a few weeks as a volunteer on a farm in India in 1970. It was attached to the Initiatives of Change centre in Panchgani, Maharashtra. At that time the farm was managed by a New Zealander, John Porteous.

Lalana Yapa

On Yapa's first day there, a room was being prepared for 200 new baby chicks. Yapa felt that the nails on the window grill were not strong enough

Vijita Yapa

and told his Indian colleague, an agriculture graduate, who took little notice. The next day two polecats got in and killed 146 chicks. 'I gloated over how I had advised the Indian, who had more experience, and condemned him.' Porteous was away on holiday at the time. When he returned he listened to the facts and then said, 'Let's be quiet and listen to our inner voice.'

After the silence, Porteous said, 'Though I was not here, I am responsible for the disaster and the chicks must be replaced.' The Indian said he was responsible and apologized for not fixing the window. This made Yapa uncomfortable, he says, because the thought that occurred to him was: 'If you felt the window was not secure, why did you not persist and attend to it? Don't blame others.' The three men jointly paid for the new chicks. 'John taught me that management means being responsible, whether one is on the job or not, and accepting responsibility when things go wrong, instead of always trying to find reasons why one is not to blame.'

It was a lesson which stood Yapa in good stead when later he was the editor of the *Sunday Times* in Colombo. The paper published a disparaging cartoon of a Sri Lankan army brigadier, who had a reputation for being a firebrand. He was so incensed that he threatened to have Yapa shot—a threat that Yapa took seriously in the context of the volatile war being waged between the government and Tamil Tiger separatists in the North, on the one hand, and Sinhala extremists in the south. The officer thought the cartoon had undermined his authority.

Taking a risk, Yapa decided to visit the brigadier at army headquarters, despite his publisher's caution. 'I came here because I am responsible for what goes in the paper,' he told the brigadier, who vented his anger in no uncertain terms. Yapa produced his passport to show that he had been abroad at the time the cartoons had been published and didn't know about them. The brigadier demanded that the paper print an apology, but Yapa refused, on the grounds that all cartoons, by their nature, are meant to be caricatures. The brigadier sued the newspaper but the judge dismissed the case.

Yapa resigned from the *Sunday Times* in 1991, following public threats from the then Sri Lankan President, Ranasinghe Premadasa. He had been angered by a regular column in the paper which appeared to criticize his relationships with his cabinet ministers. The newspaper's proprietor told Yapa to drop the column. Yapa saw this as a challenge to his editorial independence and resigned. He decided to retire from journalism and concentrate on his business.

Vijitha Yapa Bookshops which he initiated in 1992 are now the market leader in the nation's English book retailing market. His son, Peshan, is being groomed to take over the business.

The shop in Galle has been relocated to a better site, attracting more customers, and is back in profit. Yapa's elder son, Daminda, graduated as an architect from the Glasgow School of Art and has helped in the reconstruction following the tsunami, designing and implementing a project for 240 low-cost houses for the Belgian Red Cross. Galle and the nation continue in the process of restoration, and healing, following the devastating effects of the 2004 tsunami.

www.vijithayapa.com
email: vijiyapa@gmail.com

6

Giving girls a chance

*Black Monday, the devastating stock market crash of October 1987,
changed the lives of two women who founded a charity
to tackle illiteracy.*

ROYA HAYAT is one of the lucky ones. She was born in Kabul,
Afghanistan, to Pakistani parents, the fourth out of six sisters
and a brother. Her father brought the family back to Pakistan in
1989, to escape the Soviet war in Afghanistan. Roya was illiterate when, as a young girl, she joined Sayurj Public School in
Chitral, in the North-West Frontier Province, that year. Her only
language was Persian.

Now she has graduated in economics at Qurtuba University
in Peshawar and looks forward to studying for an MA in banking or management. The school in Chitral, supported with
funds from a UK educational charity, taught her English, Urdu
and Maths and transformed her aspirations. Her story is an
exceptional one in a country where, in some rural areas, only
two per cent of women are literate. In Afghanistan, the Taliban
deliberately supressed girls' education.

In the long war against poverty, 'there is no tool for development more effective than education for girls and empowerment
for women,' said Kofi Annan, speaking as the UN Secretary
General in 2004. 'No other policy is as likely to raise economic
productivity, lower infant and maternal mortality, or improve
nutrition and promote health, including the prevention of

49

Roya Hayat (front right) with other Sayurj Public School children in 1989

HIV/AIDS,' he said. 'When women are fully involved, the benefits can be seen immediately: families are healthier; they are better fed; their income, savings, and reinvestment go up. And what is true of families is true of communities and, eventually, whole countries.'[1]

The need for girl education is enormous. Till recently, over 100 million children worldwide received no primary education—60 per cent of them girls—according to the charity Save the Children. But the trend is in the right direction. In 2005, the number of children without primary education declined to about 72 million, 57 per cent of them girls, according to UNESCO statistics. However, this did not take into account the children who were officially enrolled in school but did not attend. In sub-Saharan African, 20 million girls get no education. And some two-thirds of the world's 800 million illiterate adults are women. The world paid lip-service to the UN millennium development goal of providing education to as many girls as boys by 2005, says a Save the Children report, *60 Million Girls*.[2] Yet a World Bank report states: 'Providing girls with an education boosts economic productivity, lowers maternal and infant mortality rates and reduces poverty'[3]. And UNICEF's State of

50

the World's Children Report, 2006, says that the UN's millennium development goal of universal primary education by 2015 is still achievable.

In 2006, Gordon Brown, then Britain's Chancellor of the Exchequer, pledged to spend £8.5 billion over 10 years to provide universal primary education for all. 'Now is the time for us to keep our promises,' he said. 'None is more important than the Millennium Development Goal that by 2015 every one of the world's children is able to go to school.'[4]

'Girls' education is important not just for poverty reduction,' says Ujwala Samant, Director since 1993 of the London-based educational charity Learning for Life (LFL). 'Education of girls makes a difference the world over. But in Third World countries it seems to have a more lasting, community effect than just educating young men. Boys have strictly one goal: getting a job, earning a living, taking care of the family. But women tend to think of education from the larger perspective of what impact it has on the community. It is not often males who look after the health, hygiene and nutrition of the family. Girls do that.'

Samant, originally from Mumbai, India, gained her PhD at Syracuse University, New York. Her doctoral research was on the impact that literacy has on adult women in Mumbai's slums, including how they 'socialize' their children, and how

School children in Khoj, Pakistan, supported by Learning for Life

51

they claim their rights. 'The word "rights" is not in a lot of Asian women's vocabulary,' she says. 'But girls are socialized to be care-takers, care-givers when they are very little. Girls that are given an education are more likely to make sure that their children are educated.'

Learning for Life, based in small offices in West London, supports 168 schools, mostly in Pakistan, benefiting 8,750 children. Three schools are in India. Until 2005, LFL also funded a school in Kabul, Afghanistan, with 300 children. These 'grassroots village community schools' are initiated by local people, to whom LFL donates basic school equipment, seed money and teacher training, in partnership with local non-governmental organizations.

When the devastating earthquake of 8 October 2005 hit Pakistan, over 70,000 people were killed. Twenty-five LFL-funded schools were destroyed, killing 51 children and injuring 43. Over 1,000 of the children benefitting from LFL lost their parents and their schools. Within months the charity, under Samant's leadership, had raised £280,000 towards rebuilding and re-equipping the schools.

LFL raises nearly three quarters of a million pounds a year. Its funding comes from the UK's National Lottery, the Department for International Development (DFID), private companies and trusts, and public donations. A National Lottery grant of £756,000 supports a community development project in the Indian state of Andhra Pradesh, while £430,000 helps to fund 70 schools in Pakistan's North West Frontier Province. A DFID award of £75,000 supports a schools' awareness programme within the UK. This provides resource packs to some 125 UK schools, aiming to raise awareness of different cultures following the terrorist attacks of 9/11, 2001. British school children now exchange letters with children in Pakistan.

Learning for Life, founded in 1993, was the brainchild of two women: Charlotte Bannister-Parker, who had worked on development projects in Pakistan, Nepal and India towards her doctoral thesis and Sophia Swire, who had been a stockbroker for a merchant bank in London.

Bannister-Parker, daughter of Sir Roger Bannister, the first athlete to run the mile in under four minutes, had worked in India as a research journalist and then with ActionAid in Nepal. Her thesis, at Durham University, was on the education of pre-literate women and the importance of girl-child education.

She chaired LFL's board of trustees from 2000 to 2002, and says that the charity's aim is to 'educare not just educate'. Children, especially those from Afghanistan who have suffered the psychological traumas of war, 'need education and sport, and they need love,' she told a public forum in the Initiatives of Change centre in London in 2002. Under the Taliban regime, girls' education was banned. Yet Afghani girls were so keen for an education that they risked their lives by going to secret underground schools. The school in Kabul supported by LFL had to tailor its curriculum to the local needs—including instilling into the children the dangers of unexploded land-mines. Bannister-Parker quotes the old dictum: 'If you educate a man you educate an individual; if you educate a woman you educate a whole family.'

Sophia Swire co-founded Learning for Life following a high-flying career at a merchant bank. She is never likely to forget the devastating stock market crash of 'Black Monday', 19 October 1987, which was to have a profound knock-on effect on her career.

The previous Friday, stock markets had begun to go into free fall. It was the morning of the Great Storm which devastated swathes of southern England—the worst since 1703. So many trees—some 15 million—were felled during the night of 15-16 October that London came to a standstill. Most executives were unable to reach the City at a time when Wall Street was seeing serious losses.

At the time Swire was an institutional equity salesperson, heading up the Spanish and Italian desk at Kleinwort Benson Securities. She was fresh out of university and fully expecting to break through the proverbial glass ceiling of female promotion. That morning she clambered over several enormous tree trunks to get to the City. But there was hardly any trading, so few could get to work. Instead, a friend air-lifted her out by helicopter to spend a day in the country. 'It was,' she said, 'surreal.'

The following Monday, all hell broke loose as traders tried to catch up with the situation in New York. The delay caused by the storm had a devastating effect. Black Monday went down in history as one of the 20th century's worst days for share prices, surpassing the Wall Street Crash of 1929. £50 billion was wiped off values on the London Stock Exchange, a drop of 26.4 per cent, while the Dow Jones Industrial Average fell 22.6 per cent. 'There was a cut-throat atmosphere,' Swire recalls. 'Quite a number of my friends were fired over lunchtime. They weren't allowed back in the dealing room. We found ourselves fighting for survival. We were placed under pressure to put our clients into stocks that the bank had overbought, whether or not we believed in them. I refused. Later, I had a stand-up argument in front of 500 men on the dealing room floor about a major client of mine—the Vatican—whom my boss was trying to steal from me. It's your job or mine, he told me.'

In the midst of the mayhem, Swire realized she was 'fighting tooth and nail' for something she didn't believe in. 'I realized there was more to life than making money,' she told a Channel 4 TV documentary, broadcast in 2005. 'I decided to leave the City because I felt there was pressure on me to behave unethically.'

Taking leave from Kleinwort Benson, she went for a three-week holiday to Pakistan's North West Frontier Province, to explore what she had secretly wanted to do all along: international development and journalism. 'I had always been a big traveller and adventurer. I was keen to write and wanted to make a difference. None of this was satisfied by my City job.'

She landed in Peshawar, close to the Khyber Pass and east of the Hindu Kush mountains of Afghanistan. She was drawn there, she says, by 'the romance' of the Hindu Kush as well as the Soviet-Afghan war in Afghanistan, where a number of her contemporaries had gone as correspondents and cameramen. Her brother, Hugo Swire, now a Tory MP, had set up a TV satellite facility in Peshawar 'and was full of stories of the Mujaheddin'.

In September 1988 she visited Chitral, a land-locked former

principality in the Hindu Kush, and a place of breathtaking beauty. On her first day there, her 25th birthday, she experienced a *coup de foudre*—a lightening flash of revelation. She was watching local tribesmen play 'a wild polo match against the backdrop of the incredible granite mountains which shoot 25,000 feet into the sky. I had never seen anything so beautiful, so dramatic. I thought, "This is it. This is my spiritual home."'

© Kiloran Howard

Sophia Swire with Afghani boy at LFL-funded school for Afghani children in Peshawar

After the match, the Deputy District Commissioner for Chitral, a Punjabi army major called Javed Majid, approached her. 'You are the kind of woman I have been looking for to help me set up a school here,' he said. 'Why me?' she asked. 'Well, did you go to university?' he replied. 'Yes.' 'In that case you have 15 years more education than most of the local women here.' He had tried to recruit teachers from down-country in Pakistan but it was considered a hardship posting and no one would come. He explained that he was desperate for English teachers because the language would enable local Chitrali-speaking girls, who did not even speak Urdu, to go eventually to university. 'Within one generation the standard of living of this whole valley will rise.' Swire saw this as her *kismet* (fate) and there and then agreed. Majid asked her to find other English women to join her and bring library books and school equipment. 'OK, consider it done,' she replied.

Back at Kleinwort Benson, Swire picked up her Christmas bonus and resigned. Her colleagues were shocked as she was being groomed for the top. Kleinwort Benson's chairman offered to keep her job open for a year, telling her that what she was doing was completely wonderful and totally mad. Swire says, 'The second I handed in my notice I didn't look back.' She used

Benazir Hayat

Roya Hayat in 2007

her Christmas bonus money from Kleinwort to buy schoolbooks and equipment.

Flying back to Pakistan in January 1989, she and two English friends joined Major Majid and his wife who had managed to recruit some teachers locally. Sayurj Public School opened with 40 children, aged four to 12. Four years later there were 500. Roya Hayat, one of the brightest pupils, was among them.

In 1993, a family of Afghan refugees in Peshawar asked Swire if she would help sponsor six schools for 3,000 girls in the Northwest Frontier Province. She realized that to raise the funds needed she would have to form a registered educational charity in Britain. Charlotte Bannister-Parker had been thinking on similar lines and suggested the name, Learning for Life, which they launched that year.

Swire finds it 'profoundly humbling' to visit the schools which have benefitted from Learning for Life. 'It is one of the most exciting things to see how a tiny school is changing the values of whole communities. Some children will go back to work in the fields. That's understood. But at least they will be able to read their street signs; to vote in a more mature and responsible way; to be less vulnerable to the feudal landlords who want to buy their votes. They will be more conscious and intelligent about their choices.'

A founding trustee from 1993, Swire chaired LFL's board from 1995 to 2000. But her growing pashmina fashion and documentary film businesses, founded in 1993, took up much of her time and eventually, feeling that it was time for the charity to have 'fresh energy', she and Bannister-Parker stepped down from LFL's board of trustees.[5] Bannister-Parker has since been ordained as a Church of England minister, and is now the

Assistant Curate at the University Church of St Mary, Oxford. She and her husband continue to help fund-raise substantial amounts for Learning for Life, especially following the 2005 earthquake in Pakistan.

Swire has never regretted giving up her banking career. Once, as she returned from a spell in Pakistan, where she had found 'real fulfilment', the airliner's fuselage started cracking up and the plane began falling out of the sky. 'I was 26 at the time and I remember thinking, "Thank you, God, for a fantastic life".'

She hopes the Asian children supported by LFL will be, at the very least, literate and numerate. The best of them will also be 'socially and environmentally aware and, above all, committed to sharing their advantage with those around them, as teachers, doctors, or engineers.'

Roya Hayat is one of them. Keen to share her advantages, she has taught English in the Afghani refugee school supported by LFL. 'Education,' she says, 'makes my vision broader, in a male-orientated society like Pakistan. I come face to face with people with more confidence and courage, which would be difficult without being educated.' As Swire comments, 'Education is the best means to positive long-term development.'

www.learningforlifeuk.org

Updated from article first published in For A Change magazine, December 1998/January 1999.

1. Address to Women's Health Coalition, 19 January 2004.
2. 'School's still out for girls' by Kim Sengupta, *The Independent*, UK, 5 September 2005.
3. 'Focus on Women and Development', World Bank, 8 March 2004.
4. *The Independent*, UK, 13 July 2006.
5. The fashion and home-ware brand that Swire founded, Sophia Swire London, gives five per cent of profits to childrens' charities and is run on the principles of corporate social responsibility. www.sophiaswire.com

7

Walkerswood—a Jamaican experience of social enterprise

A Jamaican community is developing a global brand—and tasting a sustainable alternative to globalization's destructive side.

NOT FAR from the birthplace of reggae legend Bob Marley, in the St Ann district of Jamaica, three young farmers are working on a pepper farm in Walkerswood village. Aston, Hopeton and Horacio are being supervised by 82-year-old farm manager Osbourne 'Apple' Francis. If they were not farming, they would have to find jobs, if lucky, in the northern coastal resort of Ocho Rios, perhaps in the tourist hotels, bars or shops of Jamaica's cruise ship destination.

Instead it is the tourists from Ocho Rios who take the drive up the hill, climbing the twisting road through Fern Gulley, to Walkerswood, population 3,000. There they visit the community's food factory which manufactures the jerk (barbeque) seasoning that has become synonymous with the flavours of the Caribbean. The Walkerswood Jerk Country Tour, around the factory and its spacious grounds, is one of the Caribbean's top 10 'community tourism' attractions. The Sandals hotel chain promotes Walkerswood to its guests, a Sandals sales representative declaring that 'there is nothing like it in the whole of Jamaica'. Visitors meet Mother Thyme in her spice garden, where her 18th century-style wattle-and-daub hut is surrounded by the herbs and spices used to prepare favourite

Mike Smith

Mother Thyme in her spice garden

Caribbean dishes. Then it is on to the factory to view the production processes and taste the products. Walkerswood is aiming to create a Jamaican international food brand and exports 80 per cent of its products.

Walkerswood's self-help projects also aim to be a model for rural development, countering the drift to the big cities in search of jobs that plagues many developing economies. The experiment attracted a Vice-Premier of China, Keng Piao, who visited in 1979, and Prince Charles in 2000.

At the heart of the Walkerswood experiment is the remarkable relationship of trust built between Afro-Caribbean entrepreneurs, including Woody Mitchell, Managing Director of the food company and winner of the Norman Manley Award for 'excellence in service to the community', and a white land-owning family that might have been mistrusted as members of the privileged 'plantocracy'.

The story goes back to the 1930s. Minnie Pringle, daughter of of one of Jamaica's largest landowners, inherited Bromley, the big colonial house standing on a commanding height overlooking Walkerswood. Her father, Sir John Pringle, had owned 50 estates including Laughing Water, where the James Bond film *Dr No* was filmed.

Inspired by a Fabian social conscience in the political ferment of the 1930s, Minnie Pringle opened Bromley to blacks and whites alike, with villagers joining in morning prayers. 'In the light of over 280 years of British colonial history, it was an incredible centre,' comments Kingston journalist Martin Henry.

One Bromley visitor was the renowned social reformer Thom Girvan, who in 1940 launched the nation's first Pioneer Club in

Walkerswood, spearheading rural development. Girvan headed up the social welfare programme of People's National Party founder Norman Manley. Walkerswood's Pioneer Club was the first development in this programme. Two villagers, Alton Henry and Peter Hinds, took up the baton. They developed the 800-acre Lucky Hill farm co-operative, the first of its kind in the Caribbean. Henry was a strong Baptist and Hinds was a natural leader, despite being illiterate.

Minnie Pringle's daughter, Fiona Edwards, now 92, and grandsons Johnathan and Roddy have continued Bromley's community tradition. Fiona says she was 'enjoying a wild life' as a teenage socialite in Britain, when she encountered the 1930s spiritual revival movement, the Oxford Group. This made her 'want to do something' to get involved in the Walkerswood community.

Her two sons inherited this social and spiritual ethos. Johnathan Edwards helped to develop the Walkerswood Community Council, launched in 1973, whilst his brother Roddy headed its unemployment committee. They were determined to create local jobs, Roddy declaring that, as a white Jamaican, he has benefitted from 'a grand theft from people who had not been paid properly for their part in the nation's development'. Like all Jamaicans, he was only too well aware of the history of slavery in a country where, at the height of the slave trade, African slaves outnumbered whites by 16 to one. 'The best way for people of European descent to be involved in reparations is to engage in sustainable, fair businesses,' he says.

He and other Walkerswood villagers launched Cottage Industries in 1976, at first selling jerk pork to the eight bars in the surrounding area. It soon became the first company to bottle and market Jamaica's celebrated jerk seasoning. Other products followed, and as markets expanded, villagers found employment in the company, renamed Walkerswood Caribbean Foods, and on the nearby farms.

But then crisis hit following a nationwide drought in 1996-97. As crops dried up, the cost of escallion (spring onions), a jerk seasoning ingredient, shot up from J$15 to J$95 per pound.

The company might not have survived but for the intervention of a new start-up banker, Peter Bunting. The son of a dairy farmer and former Peoples National Party MP, Bunting became, he says, 'captured by the Walkerswood story and the challenge of bringing employment to rural communities at a time when the commercial and the social seemed to be in conflict'.

At first Bunting had been suspicious of white Jamaicans such as the Edwards brothers. But meeting Roddy Edwards in Walkerswood and at an international conference in Caux, Switzerland, in 1994 changed his mind. Now, he was ready to take a huge risk on behalf of Walkerswood Caribbean Foods, 'at a time when it had no collateral and at a time when other banks were collapsing and being supported by the government'. At 7.30pm—and 1.30am for Roddy Edwards who was in England at the time—Bunting agreed to sign a critical guarantee of $US ½ million, despite minimum collateral from the company.

At business school, Bunting had been taught the 'five Cs of credit-worthiness', the first being Character. 'Obviously at Walkerswood they had an over-abundance of character which compensated for all the rest,' Bunting says. The support from his investment bank, Dehring Bunting & Golding Ltd, which he describes as a 'socially conscious bank', was one sixth of the bank's then total assets. 'We've stayed at the unsecured end of the business; it is at the cutting edge of risk,' he says. Moreover, 'it is not all one way traffic'. Walkerswood, he says, 'has affected my own thinking and social consciousness within my own company, in the way we treat our employees, including profit sharing and bonuses.'

He has never regretted his support for Walkerswood, not least because of its 'high value brand image', at the quality end of the market, and strong foreign exchange earnings. The company's image, logo and bottle labels, capturing the sunshine and vibrant colours of Jamaica, have been developed by artist and author Virginia Burke, whose *Eat Caribbean* was Jamaica's best-selling cook book in 2006. The brand image is also promoted at the company's Jamaican restaurant, Bamboula, in Brixton, south London, opened in 1997.

In 2005 the company invested US$6 million in a 15-acre plant, across the valley from Bromley, having received a major equity stake from Jamaican businessman Ray Chang. He stepped in as an investor after first meeting Managing Director Woody Mitchell in 1996. Peter Bunting had introduced Mitchell and Edwards to Ray Chang's sister, Thalia Lyn, and Chang had subsequently been impressed by hearing Mitchell on a radio interview.

Logistically, it might have made more sense to locate the new factory near the port in Kingston, to facilitate exports, rather than two hours away in Walkerswood. But the company was keen to maintain its commitment to community and rural development.

The ceremonial ground breaking for the new plant was performed by Jamaica's then Governor General, Sir Howard Cooke, a regular visitor to Bromley since the 1960s. Sir Howard says that, as a young Fabian socialist and politician of the People's National Party, 'I used to attack the privileged plantocracy, saying that they were not making themselves available to teach, to educate and, much more than that, to make land available. But Walkerswood was unique, in which the great house was very dominant in the life of the people, as a teaching point, as a point to create growth.' It was unusual, says Sir Howard, to find people from the 'plantocracy' understanding the social and community ethos of the great Jamaican leader Norman Manley. 'Walkerswood is an example of what spirituality can do for the people,' Sir Howard says.

The 'spirituality' is reflected in the food company's voluntary morning worship for any of the staff. On the day I visit, 15 take part in the canteen, singing 'Let the spirit of the Lord come down' and offering up extemporary prayers. 'We want this to be a place where love spreads across the nation,' declares Lesept Smith afterwards. He has worked in the packaging area for 13 years and pays tribute to the late 'Aunt' Zoë Ellis, a packaging supervisor whose idea it was to bring daily devotions to the company.

The factory now employs 160 people manufacturing 23 products, from coconut rundown sauce and solomon gundy fish paste, to chutneys, guava jam and rum marmalade.

Escallion crop being washed inside the Walkerwood factory

Equally importantly, it provides a market for some 3,000 farmers and seasonal pickers across Jamaica who supply the ingredients: scotch bonnet peppers, escallion (spring onions), ackee fruit, callaloo (spinach) leaves, Jamaican ginger, reputed to be the best in the world, and thyme among them. Walkerswood's success in the market place 'has had an economic multiplier effect throughout its community,' generating a steady income for local farmers, according to a 2005 World Bank report on the Caribbean.

The company exports 80 per cent of its output, to grocery chains and shops in the Caribbean, North America and Europe, on a turnover in 2006 of US$6 million. When I visited, the company's European marketing agent had just emailed that the UK's Waitrose chain wanted to order up to 12 products. There are huge export markets to explore, from Mexico to Spain and Australia, says the company's international sales manager, Matthew McLarty.

At the community pepper farm, the young men are growing sweet peppers, lettuces and cabbages under a 103-foot long greenhouse, in a controlled environment avoiding pesticides. The aim is to provide a year-round supply to the factory, in a project funded by USAID and the United Nations Development Programme.

Johnny McFarlane, the food company's Director of Group Development, hopes an aid agency will invest in a US$100,000 solar crop drier. Rather than subcontracting the job, the company would make an endowment, based on kilo throughput, into the Walkerswood Community Development Foundation. McFarlane had worked in real estate in Canada, but was so impressed by Walkerswood that he returned to his native Jamaica in the 1970s to join the company, taking a two-thirds cut in income.

The development foundation, the only village-focussed one of its kind in Jamaica, helps to support community activities: education, tackling HIV/AIDS, and emergency relief for reconstruction after hurricanes—the island was badly hit in 2004 and hurricanes in 2005 and 2007 caused severe damage to crops. Walkerswood is the only Jamaican village to build, in 1983, its own post office, leased to the government which in turn pays into the development foundation. The foundation's treasurer, Rupert Francis, reports that the Environmental Foundation of Jamaica has funded two biodigesters to recycle used water from the food factory to local farms.

In the village's arts and crafts building, Michael Denton and his carpentry team, Jerome and Benjamin, are making a range of products to sell in the factory's tourist shop: tea boxes, cheese boards, coasters, jewellery boxes and key racks, all inlaid with colourful ceramic tiles. Orders come from gift shops in Kingston and at the airport, and from as far as the Bahamas.

'Walkerswood is an oasis in rural Jamaica,' says Hopeton Dunn, an academic at the University of the West Indies who is Chairman of the Broadcasting Commission of Jamaica. 'It has helped to create a model community in which those who had privilege and prosperity are working alongside those who are dispossessed, in a sharing way, creating a symbol to the whole of Jamaica of what might be when there is a social conscience and collaboration.'

Communities like Walkerswood also counter the destructive side of globalization, says Doreen Frankson, one of Jamaica's leading business women who was President of the Jamaica

Manufacturers' Association, 2003 to 2007. Globalization, she says, 'has been very damaging because of opening up markets here to the world. We are struggling to be competitive. Companies like Walkerswood, that are indigenous and have a niche market, are the direction we should be going.'

She wants to see more rural agribusinesses following in Walkerswood's steps, providing 'direct and indirect employment in the community'. There are a few, but not nearly on the scale of Walkerswood. 'Their products are in high demand. They are one of the companies that really are a beacon for the rest of us.'

Woody Mitchell, wheel-chair bound since a car accident in 1972, says that Walkerwood's young farmers are finding dignity in working on the land, realizing that farming is not just for the elderly. And though unemployment is officially at 12 per cent nationally, there is no 'compulsory unemployment' in Walkerswood.

There is a lot of land and 'the easiest jobs we can create here are in farming—people actually going into the soil and producing supplies,' says Mitchell. 'But a lot of young people, especially the young men, don't want to dirty their hands. Our vision is that, with love, these young farmers—the Hopetons, Horatios and Astons of this world—can become so successful that they will be able to build their own careers and see a new profile of who a farmer is. In Jamaica, a farmer is [seen as] an old man of 60 or 70 who has dirt on his clothes. We need to change that vision.'

Mitchell too has found dignity and, he says, a divine purpose in his role at Walkerswood. He was a 25-year-old laboratory scientist at Jamaica Reynolds Mines when the car accident broke his back. The driver had gone straight over a traffic island, and the Land Rover tipped on to its side, throwing Mitchell out onto the stump of tree. At first he went through 'torrid times' at Kingston University Hospital and then in rehabilitation, knowing that he would never walk again. But seeing another paralysed man driving a car gave him the hope that he, too, could live an independent life.

He had hoped to gain a scholarship from Reynolds mines to study at university. But the company would not take him back, though they helped him to take a correspondence course in accountancy. This gave him employment, helping small business people, while he lived at his parent's property in Walkerswood.

Two years after his accident, he was in the driving seat of a station wagon with automatic gears and hand controls. Then, in the late 1970s, he got a job with Cottage Industries, making deliveries of fudge and other produce to gift shops, to earn extra cash. But it meant having someone with him the whole time and too much driving was not good for him. He had been 'petrified' at the hospital that he would end up with body sores. So it was a godsend when he became Managing Director of the fledgling company in 1983.

Mitchell characterizes his relationship with Roddy Edwards, the company's co-founder and Chairman, as 'great partners together'. 'He has his views and at times they might not converge with mine. But at the end of the day we are aiming for the same goals. Roddy and I have got on great over these years.' But there have been times when 'we have had really cross words'. Once Mitchell, under pressure, made a crucial marketing decision when he could not reach Edwards on the phone, though it was Edwards' jurisdiction. On hearing this, Edwards was so mad, says Mitchell, that 'he said he was going to resign, blah, blah, blah. Eventually we resolved it and it was for the ultimate good of the company.'

'I have asked myself so many times, "Why was my life spared?"' Mitchell says. 'Sometimes we wonder if there are no coincidences. Things happen for a reason. The truth is that I have been very fortunate to have achieved what I have in this chair. So many people have not been given the opportunities that I have. I give God thanks every day of my life; he has kept me healthy thus far.' He adds, with laughter in his voice: 'I have been sitting here for quite a long time. And I have certainly felt the Lord. So I continue to praise my God, sing him all the praise and give him all the dance, because it is through him that I am here.'

Mike Smith

Woody Mitchell, Managing Director, and Roddy Edwards, co-founder, Walkerswood Caribbean Foods: 'Great partners together'

It was at the Walkerswood community council meetings that Woody first met his wife, Pat. Throughout the food company, stability of employment has had an unexpected side effect: encouraging marriage amongst the employees, with some 10 marriages taking place. This is significant in a country where 80 per cent of children are born outside wedlock, despite the nation's strong Christian traditions.

The company has a vision that generating enough rural jobs could also prevent vulnerable young women, desperate for an income, from drifting to the cities and being caught up as drug mules in the notorious drug trafficking trade. Jamaica is a staging post between Colombia and Britain and there are more Jamaican women in British jails than any other nationality.

Edwards admits that it has been 'a huge gamble' to invest in the new state-of-the-art plant. But it was essential to meet growing global demand. In 2005, sales were up by 10 per cent, despite the hurricane, and by 15 per cent in 2006, but start-up losses at the new plant have been dauntingly high and the company is seeking new investors.

'We need to be part of a global process where business decisions are conscience-led, not merely profit driven,' Edwards says. He speaks of the critical need 'to get the balance right in resource allocation', between employee and customer needs, and between environmental sustainability and commercial imperatives. 'I believe this is best done by a team of men and

Mike Smith

Walkerswood Caribbean Foods factory

women who search their conscience for what is right as well as studying the balance sheet.' It remains to be seen whether Walkerswood will win through on this basis. But its achievements to date are real and have been an inspiration to many.

See also 'Developing local flavour', Guardian Weekly,
27 April-3 May, 2007.

8

Water for a thirsty land

*Kenyan lawyer **Joseph Karanja** tells how he found spring water on his land, which he will market nationwide.*

Worldwide 1.3 billion people do not have access to safe drinking water, according to the UN. Thirty-one countries face chronic water shortages, and by 2025 nearly 50 countries will face shortages affecting 2.8 billion people. With population growth, global demand for clean drinking water is expected to grow by 40 per cent in the next 20 years. Every initiative to secure water supplies will be necessary.

EIGHT YEARS ago I was looking for land near Nairobi to build a house. I was shown a plot that I didn't like, simply because there was no water supply. It had everything else I was looking for. Those who were already settled there bought water from vendors who brought it from far away in tankers. My immediate reaction was to say no. However, I promised to get in touch with the seller the following day.

The next morning I woke up with a strong feeling that I should buy the land and use the money for house construction to drill a borehole instead. I looked in the Yellow Pages and rang the first water drilling company I found.

I bought the plot and the driller assured me of the prospects of striking water. I will never forget the day in February 1999 when the drilling began. A group of 72 women from a Presbyterian church, who were on their way to prayers, decided to stop by and prayed, thanking God that water was coming. It took several months to drill the nearly 700-foot-deep borehole. It left me without a penny. In April 2000 everything was ready: the borehole fitted with the pump, the powerhouse with a water-selling point at the front, an office at the back, and a 20 foot tower holding two plastic tanks of 10,000 litres each.

Joseph Karanja

At this time Kenya was going through a drought that had lasted for many years. People came from near and far to buy water at my borehole. They came on donkeys, in vehicles and tankers. For two months we operated for 24 hours a day. I brought the cost of water down from 20 Kenya shillings per 20 litre jerry-can to two shillings.

My next thought was to supply my neighbours with water directly to their homes. Today, 46 homes and three schools have running water in their taps. I have employed seven people, mainly meter readers. Over 40 young men earn a living, buying from us and selling the water elsewhere. The government has asked us to bottle the water and soon we will have 'Summer Drop' mineral water in shops and supermarkets in Kenya, and possibly in Uganda and Sudan. This will mean employing at least 20 more people.

By the end of 2000, the income from water sales enabled me to put up a house where I now live, in the same compound as the well. I am expanding and early next year I will be in a position to accommodate at least 10 guests comfortably. But for me the greatest satisfaction is that I am able to meet a basic need of the community, at an affordable price.

Joseph Karanja was addressing the conference on Trust and Integrity in the Global Economy, Caux, Switzerland, August 2006.

9

Zimbabwean farmers survive on 'born again' crops

Zimbabwe has seen a collapse in its agricultural base. But a group of scientists have given small scale farmers hope in virus-free crops.

As President Robert Mugabe of Zimbabwe celebrated his 82nd birthday in February 2006, his Home Affairs Minister, Kembo Mohadi, official admitted that the country faced a dire food shortage. 'There is no grain whatsoever. Our people are actually starving,' he said on national radio[1].

Zimbabwe, once the breadbasket of southern Africa, has seen such a severe collapse in its agricultural base and economy that over five million people needed charity to prevent starvation by the end of 2005, according to the UN's World Food Programme. President Mugabe's land reforms have seen a dramatic drop in commercial maize production, leaving nearly 40 per cent of the population undernourished. Four million people have fled the country.

Poor harvests in 2002 and 2003 left millions of people needing food assistance. In 2004, Zimbabwe's farmers planted only about a third of their usual fields and the World Food Programme designated Zimbabwe as a 'hunger emergency zone'.

Yet small scale farmers have not been without hope. They are surviving partly thanks to 'born again' sweet potato plants, developed by a team of Zimbabwean scientists. The six agricultural graduates are employees of Agri-Biotech, founded by

71

Edinburgh scientist Dr Ian Robertson, the company's Chief Executive, who teaches agriculture at the University of Zimbabwe in Harare.

The plants make it possible for a 30-metre square plot to feed a family of seven all year. Farmers sell on runners to their neighbours and, during 2003 and 2004, over 30,000 people benefitted. That was just the beginning. 'Since then we have delivered direct to another 3,000 beneficiaries in two districts, as well as to a large number of beneficiaries on an emergency basis,' says Robertson. 'The multiplyer effect of them selling on to neighbours is uncalculable. In 2005 we delivered to 3,000 farmers on behalf of Care International as well as to 2,000 farmers for Save the Children Fund.' Several other non-governmental organizations funded Agri-Biotech's support for some 30 orphanages, which in turn have sold on to some 600 supporting parishioners. So far Agri-Biotech has covered eight of Zimbabwe's 56 districts, chosen by the Zimbabwe Farmers Union.

The Agri-Biotech team call the plants 'born again' because they have found a way of removing the virus that plagues sweet potato crops. In a GM-free tissue culture process, they employ cutting edge science—literally. They dissect out the 0.25mm tip of the bud, which is free from viruses and other micro-organisms, and throw the rest away. The lab team then grow the bud tip in a test tube for nine months into a virus-free plant, and keep on sub-culturing it to increase numbers.

From there they transplant the plants into plastic greenhouse tunnels and take cuttings from them. These are bought by donors, such as the Swedish Centre for Co-operation, at US$0.05 each. The Swedish aid agency has funded Agri-Biotech to supply 3,000 starter plants to 240 nursery farmers. 'We need good lab work plus good greenhouse work to deliver to good farmers,' comments Robertson, whose Edinburgh PhD is in plant tissue culture.

Unfortunately, the virus cleansing is not permanent. 'Like some Christians they can backslide,' says Robertson. 'The clean plants will inevitably pick up new viruses and degenerate.

Farmers come back to us for new clean material every few years.'

The starter plants grow in August, and are irrigated during the following months of sunshine. Many resettlement farmers have access to a well, stream or irrigation system. Each of the 240 farmers can then sell the runners to over 100 neighbours in time to plant for full growth during the rainy season, which arrives in December.

Meanwhile the greenhouse nurserymen lift the virus-free sweet potato tubers and sell them early when prices are good, at a time when neighbours are growing for 'stomach-fill' for their families. Nothing is wasted. Tubers that are too small or two big to sell at the market, or are damaged by insect pests, are fed to cattle, which love them.

Boy Ncube was one of 20 nursery-men who were trained, over three days, in nursery management and field production by Agri-Biotech's Liaison Officer Reuben Tayengwa. Agri-Biotech then supplied Ncube with 3,000 rooted cuttings of 'Brondal' sweet potato as well as 200 stakes of 'Zambezi' cassava. With the help of a small amount of organic fertiliser, Ncube grew vines to sell. Over two years, his 30 metre square plot expanded to three hectares. He has

Boy Ncube

turned his initial delivery of US$150 into sales of $16,000. This has allowed him to buy a milk cow. He is building a bricks-and-mortar house for himself and his wife, and will buy a *bakkie* (pick-up truck) to carry his tubers to market. His best field has yielded 50 tons per hectare, compared with the national average of six tons.

Nicholas Chimbwedza started farming 2.5 hectares of Brondal in 2003, after failing to get a job in town. Selling vines, fertilized with cattle manure, earned him US$150. He has recently started harvesting tubers from just 0.16 hectares and has earned $1,000. This has enabled him to buy a new pump for his field. He expects ultimately to earn over US$15,000. Dickson Gumede has 0.32 hectares and expects a harvest of eight tons on a yield per hectare of 25 tons. From sales he has earned several thousand dollars in the last two years.

Agri-Biotech's donor, the Swedish Centre for Co-operation, has estimated that, for every kroner they invest in the projects, each of Agri-Biotech's farmers have earned four kroner. 'And they have fed their own families with quality food—high protein, decent amino acids and plenty of carbohydrates. The beneficiaries are very happy,' Robertson says.

In the food emergency, the Swedish Centre contracted Agri-Biotech to deliver 1,000 plants each to another 1,000 'beneficiaries': disadvantaged orphans, old people who have lost their 'middle generation' to HIV/AIDS, and single parents. 'We delivered in September 2005 and the growth is good,' says Robertson.

In the two years 2003 and 2004, thanks to Agri-Biotech's research and donor funding of some US$300,000, the farmers cashed in $1,200,000, Robertson says. The company itself made only $50,000 but it employed, at that time, eight graduates.

The UK's Department for International Development (DFID) is 'very impressed with the excellent work and dedication of Ian Robertson and his team,' says Tom Barrett in DFID's Zimbabwe office. 'We are developing a programme in collaboration with several NGOs working in Zimbabwe and Agri-Biotech that will disseminate the improved sweet potato planting material to as many as 15,000 of the poorest households in Harare and Bulawayo. If successful, and it is possible to scale up, then we hope to support a larger programme that will reach even larger numbers in other urban and rural areas. This is a unique opportunity to help people feed themselves without requiring unaffordable external inputs.'

Due to this inpetus, eight more NGOs contracted for training and planting material in the 2006-07 season. In a crash programme, the aid agency Care alone reached 300,000 small-holders directly. The other NGOs reported that another 300,000

received plants, 'sensiti-
zation' (training) and
trouble-shooting from
the University of
Zimbabwe graduates
employed by Agri-
Biotech, some via nurs-
ery farmers and some
directly. As the average
family size is five, this
meant that three million
rural and urban family

Ian and Valerie Robertson

members had access to 'born again' sweet potatoes in 2006-07.
DFID monitors reported that sweet potato was their best and
most successful intervention, and asked to gear up with more
material for the following season. So similar numbers were
commissioned for 2007-08.

The opportunities are great and Robertson emphasizes the
huge potential in cassava crops. 'Two hundred million Africans
use cassava as a staple diet every day,' he says. 'We can produce
40 to 70 tons per hectare, with a potential of 100 tons.' It is also
a primary source of starch needed in the manufacture of a range
of products, from baked beans to adhesive tape. Building a
starch factory would offer 'a huge import substitution', and
would cost only US$50,000, Robertson estimates.

He and his wife, Valerie, who teaches microbiology at the
University of Zimbabwe, are dedicated to Africa. As research
scientists they could be earning 10 times their salaries at an
American university. Instead their faith called them to serve in
Africa, after Robertson was invited to take part in a multiracial
conference, organized by Moral Re-Armament, held at the
University in 1975. He and Valerie returned in 1977 and have
live there ever since. Robertson now speaks of 'the daily habit of
wishing to take part in God's plan for humanity', through early
morning times of silent reflection.

He emphasizes Agri-Biotech's strict ethical policy of
integrity, transparency and sincerity. Integrity, says Robertson,

means 'no cheating on expenses, no ghost journeys paid by the sponsors, no lies to farmers'. Transparency means: 'sharing our ideas with farmers; listening to their problems, history and experience; never bluffing if we do not know; avoiding political judgements; telling the truth about our own vulnerability'. And sincerity means that the company delivers the plants when promised; shares ideas on hopes for the future; lets the farmers know what the company is earning; and 'above all gets the job done whatever excuses are available'.

To find out more email: agbio@mweb.co.zw

Updated from articles first published in For A Change magazine, December 2004-January 2005; African Business magazine, December 2004; Guardian Weekly, 18-24 February 2005.

1. Reported by Jan Raath, *The Times*, London, 21 February 2006.

10

Sowing seeds of hope

Rebuilding after war—and rebuilding relationships—are keys to sustainable development says agriculturalist Paul Craig.

THE INK was hardly dry on the Dayton peace treaty that brought the Balkans war to an end when agriculturalist Paul Craig made his first visit to the Bosnian capital, Sarajevo, in 1995. 'Seventy per cent of Bosnia's livestock had been killed, eaten or stolen during the war,' leaving small farmers destitute, he says.

Craig was among the first international agricultural experts into Bosnia after the war. Agrisystems, the British agricultural development company where he worked, had been asked to advise the International Fund for Agricultural Development on how to spend $6 million in Bosnia.

'I came in over Mount Egmont and was escorted at night by a convoy of French troops across the airport, which was closed, into Sarajevo in the snow. There was no electricity and only three other guests in the Hilton Hotel. We had to use the inner stair case. If you used the outer one you were in danger of being shot by snipers sitting up in the mountains, even though there was a cease-fire.'

Agrisystems trucked in some 3,000 in-calf heifers from Austria and Germany and Craig went in with one of the first distributions. 'We unloaded the cattle on a tennis court where the farmers collected them. They really had nothing. At least they would now have milk for their children, possibly a surplus to sell, or cheese to make, and in the fullness of time they would get a calf.'

Craig and his wife, Marguerite, told me this story in their home in Hertfordshire, north of London, which has a delightful view over rolling English farmland. It is an idyll remote from the war-torn trouble spots where together they have been involved in agricul-

Paul and Marguerite Craig

tural development and post-war reconstruction for over 30 years.

When we met, in January 2004, they were packing up to leave for the Solomon Islands in the South Pacific. It was a wrench for Marguerite, having put down local roots after years of travel. 'It's harder to leave this time,' she said. 'Before, when we went to Zambia, Nigeria and Papua New Guinea, our children were with us and our parents were younger.'

In 2003 the European Union awarded Agrisystems a three-year contract in the Solomons as part of a massive €80 million aid package. The islands were plagued by ethnic violence and a breakdown in law and order, following a coup in 2000 which forced the government to call in Australia and New Zealand to restore law and order and recapture control of the government's finances.

These objectives have been achieved and Agrisystems' team has since been tackling rural development, education and inter-island transport, which had largely collapsed. Part of the task has been to set up a trust fund of €12 million to manage and provide shipping, aviation and road maintenance.

'Securing the peace and financial stability is a start,' Craig says. 'But the underlying causes of the ethnic tensions are in people's hearts and actions. Rebuilding roads, wharves, schools and classrooms with equipment is pointless unless people change.'

He was drawn to the Solomon Islands whilst on an assignment for Agrisystems, working on the national economic recovery plan. He met two Islanders 'who recognized that changing the country starts with a change of heart, attitudes and actions in individuals'. They initiated a 'Winds of Change' conference in June 2004 which has since led to a growing network of people in the Islands who want, in the phrase of Mahatma Gandhi, to 'be the change you want to see'. 'This,' says Craig, 'is where my hope lies—not in new infrastructure alone.'

Marguerite, meanwhile, has put to use her experience as a primary school teacher, setting up a special-needs department at the school where she has been teaching. There she has helped the many children who have English as a second language. The islands' 800 or so primary schools had had no new teaching materials for three years. The EU and NZAid scheme funds text books for every child and provides training for some 1,100 teachers.

Paul Craig graduated in Agriculture from Edinburgh University in 1970. A formative, if unlikely, influence came from a travelling theatre group from India, brought to Edinburgh by a grandson of Mahatma Gandhi. One of their stories was of three Indian farmers who had increased their village crop yields after settling personal jealousies and finding reconciliation. 'In the following vacation I went to India and met the reconciled brothers. A divided and starving village had been transformed. They had adopted new seeds and technology and now had a surplus. That taught me a fundamental lesson—that people's attitudes and relationships are as important as any technology when seeking to improve a situation. It also led me into international development.'

The story of Craig's own rapprochement with his father, a Glasgow businessman, is captured in a re-enacted documentary film, *What are you living for?*, made by FLT *films*. It shows how a frank conversation 'lifted an iron curtain' between them and restored their friendship.

Craig gained his Masters at the University College of North Wales and spent a year in Saudi Arabia doing agricultural research, sent there by the UK's then Overseas Development Administration. From there he went to Zambia as an animal husbandry officer, a job which tested his conviction about relationships. In front of a senior official, he blamed a local livestock specialist, Mtonga, for a faulty roof. 'I immediately knew I was wrong to humiliate Mtonga in front of our boss. But it took me three days to sum up the courage to apologize to him.' Craig says his apology helped to build the trust between them. When Craig's contract ended in 1979, the Zambian graduate who took over his post told him: 'We have grown together technically but we have also grown together spiritually.'

After Zambia, Craig faced a second formative moment in his career when he and his wife had to choose between two job offers at short notice, one with the World Bank in Nigeria and other with the UK's Department for International Development in Nepal. They were much more attracted to Nepal, but they realized that they had to 'get rid of our personal preferences and be free of them' in order to find 'God's plan', as Craig puts it. Nepal would have meant half a day's treck, a risk they couldn't take with young children if they ever became ill. It quickly became clear that they should go to Nigeria, a decision they never regretted.

It was one of Craig's largest assignments at that time in monetary terms: a livestock development project of $40 million, employing expatriates from the UK, the USA and Australia. The task was threefold: to develop a credit scheme for smallholders, to help them to fatten a million head of cattle as they moved south each year from the parched northern states; to develop 100 square mile grazing reserves for the nomadic Fulani people; and to develop large scale cattle ranches, including fencing and infrastructure, which also involved importing 2,000 tetse-resistant cattle from The Gambia. The credit scheme was so successful that Craig turned a previous default rate of 30 per cent on the loans to less than half of one per cent.

As in Zambia, human relationships were again the key in Papua New Guinea where Craig was seconded by Booker Tate Ltd in 1990 to get a loss-making poultry and crocodile farm back into profit. The farm, which employed 400 people, had a million chickens and 5,000 crocodiles. Bad management had led to the receiver being called in and relations between the management and the farm workers' union were 'diabolical'.

At first, the head of the farm workers' union didn't trust Craig, and the head of the national Trade Union Congress was hostile. Their first encounter was at a restaurant where the TUC leader was 'seriously drunk', Craig recalls. The man later apologized and respect grew between them. Craig wanted to introduce fair working practices and a wage agreement. 'The employees had been treated pretty badly, particularly the unmarried men who were living in terrible conditions. We were able to improve their showers and rooms.' It took nine months, several strikes and continual trust building to implement the wage agreement but, to Craig's great satisfaction, it was the first ever such agreement in PNG to be endorsed by both the TUC, the Ministry of Labour and the Employers' Federation.

In 1992 Craig was one of the first agricultural experts to go to Albania, after the collapse of Enver Hodja's Marxist regime. His then employer, the Dublin-based Rural Development International, sent him as the project manager of a €25 million European Union reconstruction scheme. 'When I went into the Ministry of Agriculture, there was no paper, no heating, one typewriter, and they had no experience of running anything but a centrally planned system—and that was collapsing. The state farms had no funding to continue and overnight had to be split up, creating over 300,000 new farmers with 1.5 hectares each. The government had no experience of how to handle that.'

Craig's team brought in mechanization, fertilizers and agrichemicals, and trained advisers in supporting smallholders. Now, he says, 'Albania is beginning to have a decent agricultural economy and is exporting goods to Italy and elsewhere. But the fragmented landholdings continue to mean subsistence living for many.'

Craig employed Agrisystems in Albania to advise him on mechanization, and they invited him to join the company in 1994. He became its Managing Director in 2002, but stepped down in 2003 to go to the Solomon Islands[1]. The company, with a turn-over of £5 million, is dedicated to 'challenging the causes of poverty'. Craig saw its role as 'working ourselves out of a job' by handing over to local experts.

Agrisystems, contracted by the UK's Department for International Development, took Craig to Ukraine which was facing similar issues to Albania in moving from a Soviet centrally-planned system to a market economy. Ukraine was historically the breadbasket of central Europe, and has 45 per cent of the world's best soils—though only an agriculturalist could describe them as 'mouth-watering', as Craig puts it.

The £3 million, three-year project was to set up agricultural and rural development advisory centres in an *oblast* or province of 5.5 million people. They have now been handed over to Ukrainians. The country's small farmers are now able to pay towards the advice they receive, and this makes the centres, which the government cannot afford to fund, sustainable.

Meanwhile, in Sierra Leone Agrisystems has trained ex-combatants—from both the rebel forces and the Sierra Leone army following the civil war there—in rural development schemes. These include brick- and road-making, building police stations and health clinics, and training in agricultural skills. 'We insisted that half of each training course should include people who had stayed at home in the community,' Craig says. He likens integrating the rebels back in this way to the father's welcome to the prodigal son in the Biblical parable. The approach seems to be working. Clare Short, who was the UK's minister for international development, visited the project twice and was 'very excited by it,' Craig says.

Craig describes himself as a 'free marketeer', and at a public meeting in London in 2003 he didn't mince his words about the need for the European Union and the USA to end their agricultural protectionism. 'The protectionist lobbies are self-serving. Europe is two-faced: the major donor of development aid but also the originator of the most restrictive tariff barriers.'

Craig reflects that 'if you embark on a life of faith and purpose you fall often. It is important to have a partner who loves you and helps you get back on track.' He clearly has this in Marguerite. She has had a passion for teaching in primary schools for over 20 years—in Africa, the UK, Papua New Guinea and the Solomon Islands. 'As well as learning language and maths skills, children need to learn how to care for others, to share and take turns and to stand up for what they believe to be right,' she says. Each generation, comments Paul, has to learn these basic lessons afresh. 'In terms of human relationships we've all got to learn them again and again.'

Updated from an article first published in For A Change *magazine, June-July 2004.*

1. After 11 years as a director and shareholder of Agrisystems, Craig and his fellow shareholders sold the company in 2005 to a larger global development company, enabling the younger staff to take greater responsibility and releasing the older cadre, Craig says, to pursue wider agendas. He and his wife returned to Britain in 2007.

11

At loggerheads with the corrupt

After laying down his guns, Joseph Wong is working for a corruption-free logging industry in the Solomon Islands.
John Bond *tells his story.*

JOSEPH WONG was practically born into the logging industry. A Chinese-Malaysian from the island of Sarawak, he grew up in a community heavily involved in the industry and, as soon as he reached adulthood, that became his occupation.

First he worked in Sarawak. But as the logging opportunities dwindled there, he looked to the Pacific, where Chinese-Malaysians dominate the industry. Soon Wong found employment with a Malaysian logging company in Papua New Guinea and, after a few years, formed his own company.

Tragically, the logging industry is a major driver of political corruption, environmental destruction and social instability in many Pacific countries. Logging companies often get their way by bribing officials and making agreements with uneducated villagers, then stripping their land of forests for a fraction of their worth. If difficulties arise, money is usually the first method of persuasion and, if this fails, there are stronger methods. 'I had five guns,' says Wong, 'and my driver was a former army sergeant. If we couldn't get our way by money, we used force.'

In 1999 Wong was working in the Milne Bay province of Papua New Guinea where he had established Milne Bay Industries. There was to be a regional Initiatives of Change conference in Sydney, Australia, and one of the organisers invited Wong to go. In the event he was one of 28 delegates from Milne Bay to attend.

Steve Donovan

'The care I received during that conference made me realize that this world is a lot better than I thought,' Wong recalls. 'I felt I had a real home, where I could share my pain and hurt. The way of life that was being discussed of love, honesty, unselfishness opened my heart and filled the

Joseph Wong

emptiness. I felt able to talk about the way I was living. I felt purified, and started to listen to the voice deep within me.'

He returned to Papua New Guinea and got rid of his guns. He then calculated the amount of money out of which he had defrauded the tax authority. It came to one and a half million kina, at that time the equivalent of US$600,000. Two years went by before he found the courage to go to the tax officials and admit his fraud. The authority decided not to prosecute, and he repaid this sum in instalments over two years. He cancelled a licence he had obtained by bribery.

These steps opened the eyes of the Papua New Guinea authorities to the methods of the logging companies, and they set up an inquiry, which roused the resentment of other logging companies. He was no longer welcome at their meetings and parties.

This hurt him. But his new approach to life opened up other avenues. 'In the past, I despised people in prison. Now I realized that if I could change, so could they. They could become responsible citizens and build a better country. So once a week I would go to the local prison, have a meal with the prisoners, and we would talk.'

Back at the Forestry Department, Wong started encountering difficulties. He was told he must make an appointment for every visit. When he asked for an appointment he was questioned at length. Then his work permit, which had been regularly renewed for 12 years, was delayed month after month. The message was clear. Some people wanted him to leave.

He decided to make a fresh start elsewhere. He moved to the Solomon Islands to become Managing Director of Sylvania Plantation Products Ltd (SPPL), a company working in logging and palm oil production, owned by a Malaysian parent company. He was allocated 38 per cent of the shares in SPPL.

He adopted three principles—transparency, local participation and sustainable development.

Transparency was the first challenge. When he went through the company's records, he discovered many dubious transactions and missing files. He went to the government department, told them he believed there had been wrongdoing, asked their help to find the missing information, and offered to pay whatever the firm owed. These steps started to build trust between him, the department, the other shareholders, and the Solomon Islanders on whose land his company was working.

He then worked out how the landowners could gradually increase their stake in the company. 'As investors, we have a timeframe in which we expect to receive an adequate return. After that, I believe the company should be handed over to local people so that they can use the infrastructure, develop the business, and bring long-term benefit to the country. I do not believe that foreigners sitting in an air-conditioned office should decide on long-term projects far away,' he says.

SPPL was included in the listing of his parent company on the Kuala Lumpur Stock Exchange, along with three other logging companies they owned in the Solomons. Wong believed that the four companies should be locally owned.

He called a special Annual General Meeting seeking shareholder approval to transfer them to the Solomons, but failed. 'I then offered to buy the majority of shares in the four companies. We agreed a price and the sale went through in June 2005. Now I am transferring the four companies to the Solomon Islands, appointing local people as directors, and I will offer the shares for sale to Solomon Islanders.' This is a courageous move, because he is well aware of the extent of corruption in the Solomons.

'The Solomon Islands New Forestry Bill, which regulated forestry, was never even approved by the cabinet, such is the power of the logging industry,' he points out. 'And we constantly see imported logging machinery mysteriously exempted of duty. When I challenged this, the Solomon Forest Association put pressure on our buyers to refuse to deal with us.'

As a result of his stand, landowners are turning to him for advice in their negotiations with logging companies. 'I advise them to start by asking what the company will do to restore the land once logging has finished.' This has provoked strong opposition from the logging industry, and he has had to withdraw from the Solomon Forest Association. He received an anonymous threat that his house would be burnt down, but this has not stopped him. 'It is pointless to go on making a few people rich and many poor,' he says.

Wong is now working to build a team of business people who will develop a climate of integrity in Solomon Islands commerce.

First published in For A Change magazine, February 2006.

12

Life after subsidies

*New Zealand farmer **Garfield Hayes** tells of the sources of
inspiration which helped him to cope when farm subsidies
were cut overnight.*

MY WIFE and I have a family farm in the South Island of New
Zealand, 100km from Mount Cook. We own 865 hectares. In the
summer we have nearly 10,000 sheep, 100 beef cattle and 100
hectares of barley and lucerne crops.

We farm with two and half permanent employees—I'm the
half—but use the services of many agricultural specialists—
people who dip, spray, shear and pregnancy test sheep, and
other contractors who spray seed and fertilize our paddocks, by
truck and plane.

I spent over 12 years abroad in voluntary work. But when I
was 30 I had an increasing conviction to return to New Zealand
to take responsibility for the farm that my father had left me.

What were the challenges? My back was not 100 per cent; I
had never received agricultural university training; farm product prices were depressed and, shortly after my return, we were
snow-bound for three weeks, with one metre of snow and with
all our animals living outside to feed. Four days after the snow,
we had reached all the stock by bulldozer or helicopter with
feed. Regular exercise greatly improved my back.

Amazingly product prices went through the roof two years
after we returned. This covered many of my mistakes and

Garfield and Helen Hayes on their farm

helped me to set up on a good financial footing.

My father, still living on the farm, was completely blind. After four previous operations for glaucoma, he reluctantly accepted one more for a cataract removal. To his astonishment, he regained 90 per cent of his sight—in his words a miracle. He could see his wife and children for the first time in 10 years and threw away his white stick.

I was on the National Council of the New Zealand Farmers Federation when the Labor government decided to drastically change the economy. A 10 per cent goods and service tax was introduced. The New Zealand dollar was floated, the reduction of tariffs was started, and, overnight, all farm subsidies terminated. We were receiving 20 per cent of our income from the New Zealand taxpayer. Our farmers marched in the streets, but as one of their leaders I knew in my heart that New Zealand had no alternative. We exported 90 per cent of our agricultural production and our trading partners had threatened us: remove subsidies or face tariffs.

The next years were difficult. Some farmers, big and small, lost their farms. Some committed suicide. I worked so hard my hips wore out. We survived by selling a city property we had been led to purchase when we were receiving subsidies. But the fact was that we were overproducing a product that was hard to sell.

During the past 20 years there has been an enormous turn

around. New Zealand's sheep population has fallen from 70 to 40 million. Farmers have had to become very innovative. Where possible, besides producing prime lambs, they have diversified into dairying, dairy support, cereals, venison, and trees. Financial rewards have fluctuated from excellent to, at this moment, very bad. But nowhere do you hear calls for the return of farm subsidies.

During these experiences, the easy option was to purchase farm advice from specialists, but by far the most secure, satisfying and stimulating daily advice came from my early morning times of silent reflection. If God could steer us through such changes, I am convinced that he can supply the answer to the problems and challenges of world agriculture, if we choose to listen to him.

For instance, for 20 years we baled our wool in jute packs instead of synthetic packs, helping to stimulate trade with the jute growers of Bangladesh. To keep things transparent all our farm sales go through the company books.

Historically there has been division between farmers and trade union leaders in our meat processing industry. My wife, Helen, and I have met these leaders, had them to stay in our home and arranged meetings with local farmers.

Alcoholism is a big problem among our sheep shearers. Although contravening custom, we ran an alcohol-free wool shed. But with Helen giving excellent meals, the shearers were always keen to return.

In a global world, where the need for change and innovation is always constant, for New Zealand agriculture there has definitely been economic viability after the removal of subsidies.

First published in For A Change magazine, October/November 2004, from his speech to the international Farmers' Dialogue, Caux, Switzerland, July 2004.

13

Leading ethical practice—key to a good bottom line

Senior public sector manager **Ron Lawler** *tells how a commitment to honesty helps to 'raise the ethical floor'.*

ETHICAL PRACTICE is important because doing the right thing is important. Ethical practice makes possible the highest level of teamwork and effective, productive work practices, because it makes us credible.

Credibility has this effect because it engenders loyalty, the open sharing of ideas between workmates, and a greater capacity to build on the strengths of each person. These are fruits of trust.

I would go so far as to say that my effectiveness as a leader and public sector manager is determined more by my credibility than the authority that comes from the delegated responsibilities of my position.

We face the emergence of an increasingly globalized economy, society and culture. Governments cannot shirk decisions about how we respond and engage with globalization, but it is happening, like it or not.

This prospect raises many fears about what the impacts will be and where they will fall. There are also fantastic opportunities to build a world with a greater sense of shared destiny.

So how are we to engage? How can you and I as ordinary people contribute to outcomes of global justice, social responsibility, healthy environments and financial viability?

Attracta Lagan of KPMG, the accountancy and consultancy firm, suggested to businesses a few years ago that one of their tasks was to 'raise the ethical floor below the global market place'. That is 'floor'—not 'flaw'!

She describes some key principles to help raise the ethical floor which include:

- Accepting you have a choice (This is very important as we so often become locked into cynicism, finding a miserable comfort that must be broken free of);
- Changing from the inside out;
- Engaging hearts and minds;
- Standing up to be counted.

Whether we work in the public, private or community sectors, or at home, we can each play our part in this enterprise. I have worked in all of them.

In the public sector, our financial bottom line is determined differently from the private sector. We are not concerned with profit but we must live within a budget.

There are some particular aspects of ethics that are more important in the public sector, such as procedural fairness and an avoidance of, or openness about, conflicts of interests. However, the ethical and moral dilemmas or opportunities are essentially the same wherever we are.

What can assist us to negotiate those challenges is also the same. I have come to rely on ideas that come in times of quiet in the early morning or while I am walking to work. Such ideas may also be at work, if I can just stop long enough from following busy, instant responses. They can be right but they can be very inadequate. They need to be tested.

When tested on your spouse or your workmates they may prove fine or foolish, or are developed into something better.

I always thought I was more or less an honest person, thanks to my parents and what I learnt through early church years. If I was a bit naughty at least I felt uncomfortable about it!

Ron Lawler with his wife, Cynthia

When I was 22 years old I found another level of liberation, as I listened to that inner voice that has a way of letting me know things quietly.

The idea came to apologize and pay back to my employer for what I had stolen from his warehouse. I did this though I felt really stupid as the amount was so small. (It is amazing how when I do something dishonest it does not seem to be as significant or bad as when someone else does it.) My boss was aware that lots of stock was 'walking out' of the warehouse. He responded by saying, 'At last I have found someone who is honest.' He offered me a supervisory position in the company.

This experience taught me that free from the small compromises your authority and passion to tackle the big challenges increases. It set firm foundations for my engagement in the sometimes difficult task of raising the ethical floor in some workplaces I have worked in.

I am grateful for the excellent systems in place in the public sector that at least encourage honesty. However there is that attitude at large in the community which suggests that whatever you can deprive the government of is morally justified.

I have had responsibility to approve travel claims in my jobs. On one occasion a couple of people wanted me to agree to a claim for payment that was not valid. I thought, and said to them, 'You are putting me in a bad situation. I would not be able to lie straight in bed if I do what you ask.' They bid a hasty retreat and it actually helped them to trust me on all matters, though I remained watchful of them!

People who are 'bean counters' instinctively say 'no' to whatever is proposed if it looks to be a little outside the norm and a bit risky. They guard the money as if it were their own. I do not suggest that this is all bad. Checks and balances are very important.

There was a classic case of 'bean counting' in the TV comedy series *Yes, Minister*, some years ago. The government officials decided that the cheapest way to run a flash, new hospital was to employ no staff nor provide any services! That, of course, could not happen in real life.

Now, at least, many government agencies seek to focus on outcomes, like effective delivery to clients: hospitals helping the sick to get well, for instance.

There was someone in our office of equal rank to me, who had some control over the purse strings, whom I would have described as a bean counter.

One day an opportunity arose where I felt it was fair to spend some of his administrative money to assist a community to conduct a certain development event. It was unorthodox but I had read the guidelines on expenditure and found them to be silent on the particular matter.

There was a good case to justify the expenditure. However, I felt that this was one of those times to be silent and seek for a greater wisdom in dealing with this issue. It seemed clear to me that the important thing was to stick to the issue and not play the man, backing him into a corner.

His reaction to my request was, as I expected, 'No'. He claimed there was a document separate from the guidelines that made what I wanted to do impossible to justify. I asked him to provide the document to me as I needed to know for the future.

He did not produce any document and I kept insisting on seeing it. I felt like accusing him of making it all up. Finally, he announced that he had found a way to do what I had proposed to fund. I never did see any document but I believe that we were able to do the right thing by the community involved. As important, my working relationship with that person was not damaged and, in fact, contributed greatly to cohesion in the office.

I am not a natural leader according to the images I have had of leadership. I have always thought of a leader as the one who is up front expounding the vision and telling people what to do. I have discovered that leadership comes in many forms and it comes as you try to be led by the still, small voice of calm.

Our personal choices help to raise that ethical floor. The change that comes from within propels us into leadership.

You can't win them all. But for the most part people will want to go with you and work with you, even if sometimes after a struggle. The results will be an effective, creative, collaborative, satisfying life at work, and a sustainable bottom line.

Ron Lawler is a senior regional manager with an Australian state government agency, and has had extensive experience in the public and community sectors. He has been involved for many years in Aboriginal Affairs and has particular expertise in strategic planning, advocacy, community and services development. This chapter is taken from a talk he gave at an 'Australia as a neighbour' conference held in Melbourne, January 2007.

14

Workers' butterfly that aims to start a whirlwind

A leading apostle of employee ownership sees worker-owned companies as a model for sharing wealth and creating community.

THE HISTORIC date of 11 September 2001 holds special significance for the Scottish businessman David Erdal. '9/11' has become shorthand for the world's most infamous act of terrorism. It also happened to be the day that Erdal became Managing Director of Baxi Partnership Limited. Owned by a trust, this £20 million fund supports small and medium sized companies wanting to transfer ownership to their workforces, as employee-owned companies.

There is an analogy with 9/11 here, for Erdal, one of Britain's leading advocates of employee ownership, promotes an alternative to the corporate terrorism of financially-driven takeovers, asset stripping, rationalization and redundancies, which too easily destroy whole communities and leave employees bereft.

'How can companies and enterprises best serve the communities in which they are situated?' he asks. Family businesses, in particular, often have a commitment to the communities where they have grown, providing local employment and wealth. But what happens when, after several generations, the family owners want to withdraw their stake? Can they do so without jeopardizing the company's independence and local loyalties?

This was the challenge Erdal faced at the Tullis Russell paper company in Fife, where he was Chairman.

The answer is to make the employees the owners. Erdal argues that employee-owned companies serve the wider community better than those that are remotely owned by shareholders. It is a 'natural way of sharing the wealth', he says.

'All the evidence is that companies become more productive once the employees become involved,' he says. Companies where managers own shares can expect a 12 per cent increase in productivity. But companies where the entire workforce are the owners see a massive increase of over 17 per cent, says Erdal, quoting a Harvard economist's study in the UK. The wealth generated benefits the whole community where the employees and their families live. So it is a model of ownership worth backing to the hilt.

Erdal was Chairman of Tullis Russell, the prestigious family paper making business in Markinch, Scotland, from 1985 to 1996. He instigated the leveraged buyout of the company's ownership from the family members to the employees. The hand-over was completed in 1994, and Erdal reckons that, even with a slowdown in the world economy following 9/11, each of Tullis Russell's 900 employees have seen their share value in the company grow to some £6,000 to £7,000, without having to put their own savings at risk.

Tullis Russell is now owned entirely by the employees and trusts for their benefit. It has retained its reputation as one of Europe's leading specialist paper makers, outperforming the rest of the UK paper-making industry in difficult times. The company makes premium coated and uncoated printing papers, as well as paper for postage stamps and for decorating ceramics.

Tullis Russell was founded in 1809, with simple beginnings in an old flour mill. The Russell family owned the company for four generations. It now has three plants in Britain and one in Korea, and exports half of all that it produces.

Sir David Russell, who became chairman in the early 1930s, had a strong paternalistic commitment to the workforce and the community they represented. Sir David's grandson, David Erdal, was keen to maintain the firm's ethos of community involvement. He was attracted to the idea of employee ownership at a time when other family members wanted to extract their capital in order to support other business activities.

Erdal instituted a profit-sharing scheme as soon as he became chairman in 1985, whereby 7.5 per cent of the profits are used to distribute shares annually to the workforce. The shares go equally to all the employees.

In 1994, Tullis Russell, with the help of Edinburgh merchant bank Noble Grossart, set up the new statutory Employee Share Ownership Plan as part of a major capital reorganization. Around 25 family members surrendered their remaining 55 per cent stake, worth £19 million, in exchange for loan notes. These were redeemed over the subsequent years and converted into shares for the workforce as the money became available to buy them through the annual profit sharing bonus. The shares have been distributed by the statutory Employee Share Ownership Trust.

An Employee Benefit Trust acts as a market maker, for workers to trade their shares, whilst also building up a substantial long-term holding to provide stability for the whole enterprise. The scheme, building on the profit sharing bonus, depends on good annual results, which the company has achieved despite a fluctuating pound and an industrial environment that has forced many UK mills to close.

But Erdal also emphasizes that employee ownership is no substitute for good management. 'What really makes a company work is how people behave and relate to each other,' he says. 'If management behaves aggressively, owning shares in the company doesn't solve the problem. On the other hand, share ownership does provide a positive background for good management and good relations to prosper. Clearly, there is something about providing job security, and protection from the take-overs and greed which outside ownership often brings, that enables a company to be very fertile in the development of new products.'

Could the family have got a higher price by selling out to a competitor? Erdal denies there is philanthropy in the ESOP plan. 'The net benefit to the family would not necessarily have been higher because the legislation gives significant tax advantages when you sell to the employees,' he says. But he adds: 'Owning a company is different from owning any other piece of property. You can sell a table and it doesn't affect anyone. But if you own a company you are involved in a community of people.' Passing over the power that goes with ownership 'without paying attention to the interests of the people in that community,' is irresponsible, he says. 'You have to take the interests of the employees very seriously indeed.'

The ESOP satisfies Erdal's own ideals. Ever since childhood he has searched for ways to create a more just society, he says. 'I was born into a wealthy family, owning a paper mill and living in a magnificent house on top of a hill. When I went to school I made a lot of friends who were poor. At the age of five or six I didn't understand these things. One day I went with one of my friends to her home. I was appalled at what I saw and I date my interest in improving the system from that vivid experience.'

After studying Chinese at Oxford, he travelled to California where he joined a Buddhist monastery. He returned to Britain, not to join the company but the Workers Revolutionary Party. He was on the picket lines with the builders during their 1972 national strike. But it was his experience teaching in Mao's China which undermined his faith in communism. For the first 10 months there he was reinvigorated in his belief in revolution as the way forward. But then he faced the fact that 'the whole system of dictatorship was very anti-human. People were living in terror.'

Back from China, Erdal joined the family firm at the age of 29, encouraged by his late uncle, Dr David Russell, who was then Chairman. At first, Erdal admits, he didn't feel 'legitimate' coming in just because he was a family member. But gaining his MBA at Harvard Business School gave him confidence, he says. He had spells on the shop floor and in export sales before joining the board in 1981.

Erdal now holds that a competitive free market is the best system for allocating goods and services: 'It is generally honest. You buy the best products and services at the lowest price and there is no hypocrisy in it.' But he still speaks passionately against what he sees as unjust systems of ownership. Those who already own an asset, such as a family business, have the collateral to borrow money for new investment. They then receive tax breaks designed to encourage investment. But this serves to concentrate wealth in the hands of those who already have it. Non-owning employees all too easily remain in a sub-servient relationship, he argues.

His uncle had put voting control of the company into the charitable Russell Trust at a time when he had no obvious heir apparent. Managers, rather than family members, formed the majority of trustees, with the charge of keeping the company independent and serving the interests of the employees.

The obvious way of doing this, as Erdal's relatives wanted to withdraw their stake, was to set up the ESOP. Erdal was particularly influenced, he says, by visiting the Mondragon co-operatives in Spain, inspired by a Roman Catholic priest in the early 1950s. There the emphasis was based on the social doctrine of the Catholic Church that capital should serve labour rather than the other way round.

Another input came from Erdal's participation in the Caux Conference for Business and Industry in Switzerland, in 1991, where industrialists, trade unionists, bankers and businessmen were conferring on 'How management, labour, government and capital can work better together'. It came just at a point when he was facing apparent opposition to his ideas for the ESOP from two non-executive directors as well as from the convenor of shop stewards who, Erdal thought, regarded the ESOP as a 'con-trick' to undermine his authority. At Caux, Erdal was particularly struck by reading a book on industry which quoted Bill Jordan[1], then President of Britain's engineering workers' union, as saying, 'Working together is the most powerful tool for prosperity there is.'

In a time of reflection, Erdal thought about the two directors,

David Erdal

whom he had decided to sack on his return home. 'The suggestion came into my mind, I know not from where, that I should go and talk to them and listen to them. I did this and had two of the most fantastic days I've ever had. I found that these directors had done their analysis and were very well motivated towards what we were trying to do—not with the ideas I was thrusting at them. We agreed on how to develop the business in a very strong way. Similarly with the trade union convenor, I had listened to rumours and had misinterpreted his behaviour without talking to him. Now I found he was genuinely trying to find the best way to resolve problems and deal with issues on the shop floor, a key part of the whole enterprise.'

The work force at Tullis Russell, initially suspicious, subsequently became enthusiastic about the idea of being the owners. Erdal estimated that, on the firm's projected performance share-owning employees stood to be, on average, about £16,000 better off.

In 1996, David Erdal handed over the chairmanship of Tullis Russell to non-executive director Howard Browning. Erdal, meanwhile, took the gospel of ESOPs to Eastern Europe. Through Job Ownership, the precursor of the Employee Ownership Association, he and its Executive Director, Robert Oakeshott, helped several companies in Slovenia and other Central European countries to be privatized into majority employee ownership. Erdal remained a non-executive director of Tullis Russell till 2004.

The Baxi Partnership Trust has operated since 2001 as a trust-owned investment fund with the purpose of 'fostering the employee ownership of successful businesses with partnership cultures'. The £20 million trust emerged after the forced sale of the Baxi central heating boiler company, itself a former employee owned company. And here lies a cautionary tale.

Philip Baxendale inherited the leadership of the Baxi heating company in the 1950s and built it up from 70 employees to 1,200 when he retired in 1983. The company was valued at £50 million but Baxendale and his cousin sold it to an employee trust for a mere £5 million, an extraordinary act of generosity, says Erdal. In the late 1990s the CEO fell for an ill-advised £500m City-inspired acquisition. It led to the company's forced sale to a venture capital group and the employee ownership ended.

Erdal warns that, however motivated the workforce are as owners of their own enterprise, companies still need to be well managed. He emphasizes 'the importance of well-motivated managers with a concept more than their own personal bank balance'.

Baxi Partnership, based in Dunfirmline, Fife, is the phoenix out of these ashes. In its first three years it made substantial long-term loans to the all-employee buyouts of five enterprises. The loans, up to a maximum of £2 million, go into setting up company employee trusts, which buy the company and will always hold at least 50 per cent of the shares. This has the virtue of giving stability to the employee-owned company as well as acting as an internal market for employees to trade their shares. Over time each company passes out free shares to each employee, using then-Chancellor Gordon Brown's tax efficient Share Incentive Plan.

Take, for instance, Loch Fyne Oysters, an hour north of Glasgow, which cultivates oysters and mussels and smokes fish, exporting them to 22 countries. The company also started, then hived off, a popular chain of seafood restaurants (Loch Fyne Restaurants) whilst maintaining its own popular Oyster Bar and shop at Loch Fyne. The major shareholder died suddenly and the company was put up for sale. Several large food processing firms put in bids. But the workforce of over 100 wanted to keep the ownership local, to avoid the risk of asset stripping by an outside company or subsequent closure. Baxi Partnership invested £2 million in a 15-year loan at seven per cent interest.

Andrew Lane, Managing Director of Loch Fyne Oysters, says Baxi Partnership's investment has benefitted the company hugely. 'Without them we would not be in existence,' he says. There had long been an ambition to put the ownership in the hands of the workforce. 'We could only see the staff having to hock their houses and cars to get involved before Baxi came along. Baxi offers a totally different route for well run companies. It is very exciting.'

The first company to benefit from a Baxi grant, in April 2002, was Aberdeen-based Woollard and Henry where 24 employees make the dandy rolls that imprint watermarks in paper. Some 45 per cent of production is exported worldwide. The third generation of family owners had no obvious successor. So they approached Erdal to help transfer ownership to the employees through a £1 million long-term loan. 'What Baxi Partnership encourages is to have a partnership culture,' says Managing Director Fred Bowden. The two employee directors who sit on the board 'play a very valuable role,' he says. 'If people can come up with ideas they are more committed to making it happen.'

Interest on Baxi loans, at around 10 per cent plus fees, is way below the typical 30 per cent expected by venture capitalists, Erdal pointed out. 'The aim of the trust is not primarily to make a profit but to help employees acquire their companies rather than live under the thumb of other people, or under the control of outside shareholders.' He adds that 'people who sell their companies to employee buyouts like this can sleep easy at night, knowing they have not sold out their employees but left them in charge of their own destiny.'

Erdal believes that employee ownership can work at any size of company, provided that the managers strive to ensure that each person feels really involved. This may be easiest at a relatively small size, say up to 200. There are, of course, much bigger examples. The John Lewis Partnership has over 60,000 employees, or 'partners', and is one of Britain's most successful retailers. But when employees at United Airlines in the USA acquired 55 per cent of the company's shares, the management and unions failed to develop an inclusive culture and the airline had to refinance, reducing the employee stake to about 20 per cent.

In April 2007, Erdal handed over to a new managing director at Baxi Partnership, John Alexander, freeing Erdal to write a book about employee ownership. By then Baxi Partnership had helped seven companies to transfer to employee ownership, with an eighth about to complete. It is just the beginning in 'spreading the virus' of employee ownership, Erdal says. But he sees signs that 'the world is moving in this direction'. The Employee Ownership Association now has 40 member companies in the UK, including household names such as the John Lewis Partnership, Unipart and the engineers Arup Associates. And homecare businesses, which care for the elderly and infirm in their homes, have 'outstanding performance ratings', Erdal says.

Employee owned companies still represent a small minority. But Erdal believes that employee share ownership 'could become the general model. It is a much more natural way of organizing our lives, of sharing the wealth. We are a butterfly beating its wings, hoping it will turn into a whirlwind. But that will take two or three generations.'

See also 'Fife firm adopts new ownership plan', The Herald, Glasgow, 17 April 1995; and 'The boardroom revolutionary', For A Change magazine, April/May 1995. A fuller account of David Erdal's life, written by Maureen Cleave, was published in the Telegraph Magazine, London, 4 October 1997.

1. Bill Jordan became Secretary General of the International Confederation of Free Trades Unions and is now Lord Jordan.

15

The man who set out to change the media

Bill Porter founded a global media ethics campaign out of his concern about the media's influence.

'IF YOU are thinking that way why don't you do something about it?' The words, spoken to publishing executive Bill Porter by his wife, Sonja, remained ringing in his ears. When she died unexpectedly and tragically young, three weeks later, her words came back to him with the force of a command. They were a trigger, he says, to 'do something' about the influence of the media.

The first trigger, which had prompted his concerns, was when he read an article in the *Financial Times* that year, 1990. The communications industry in all its manifestations, including the mass media, had become the largest industry in the world, it said. That may be so, Porter thought to himself. But was it the most responsible? Did it always consider its moral or ethical impact on its audiences? The answer, he thought, had to be no. It was not just the sex, sleaze and scandal in the media that worried him, but rather a conviction that the media had a crucial role in building a free and just society, yet rarely turned the searchlight on itself or its methods.

Porter admitted to himself that his motivation, as the chief executive of a leading academic and business publishing house in London, 'had been primarily to make money and to become important, both for my company and myself'. And whilst these were not wholly bad motives, 'they lacked the balancing element of responsibility'. With some trepidation—'not wishing to be rejected or laughed at'—he approached colleagues in the publishing world and was surprised to find in some a similar degree of concern about the media.

Porter launched the International Communications Forum (ICF), a media ethics campaign, in 1991, three years after his retirement from publishing. He was 70 years old at the time and he chaired the ICF for the next 14 years, regarding this as the crowning fulfilment of his career.

ICF's first conference was held in Caux, Switzerland, in 1991 with Porter's colleagues—such as Gordon Graham who had been Chief Executive of the Butterworth Press and Chairman of the Publishers Association in Britain—taking part. The aim was to 'build a worldwide network of men and women in the media who believed in ethical values and applied them in their lives'. They would be responsible for the honesty and integrity of their output. It would be a 'conscience to conscience' activity, rather than an academic body. As the British journalist and feature writer Graham Turner put it at that first gathering: 'If we are blowing the whistle on others, let us make sure that our own whistles are clean.'

Porter had founded the British arm of the legal and professional publishing multinational Kluwer in 1970. It was Europe's largest law publisher and Porter was taken on to head its expansion into Britain as Managing Director of Kluwer Publishing, based at first in small offices in Brentford, west London. It eventually widened into 14 sister companies and imprints. In 1984 he was appointed Deputy Chairman of Kluwer UK, by then at its Kingsway, London, headquarters. The following year he became Chairman of the Law Panel of the Publishers Association and a national committee member of the Periodical Publishers Association.

The panel's highest profile issue was to come out in support of Salman Rushdie's freedom of expression during the *Satanic Verses* affair, following the burning of Rushdie's book by Muslims in Bradford, Yorkshire. 'In the interests of freedom of expression and freedom to publish, we supported its appearance,' Porter wrote in his memoires, *Do something about it*[1]. But the panel also urged that publishers should be more careful in future.

Blair Cummock

Porter himself agreed with Zaki Badawi, then Chairman of the Imams and Mosques Council of Britain who, shown the manuscript before publication, commented that he would not oppose the book if some pages were expressed in a more moderate language. Had senior executives at Rushdie's publishers taken heed, the whole affair might never have arisen, Porter believed.

Bill Porter

It was issues like this that encouraged him to make one focus of the ICF to be on the Western media's approach to the Islamic world. Since its launch, ICF has held 28 events around the world, involving over 2,500 media people from 114 countries. A major conference which the ICF helped to organize in 1999 was hosted by the *Financial Times* at its London headquarters. It was chaired by Lord Nolan, who had been the first Chairman of the government-initiated Committee on Standards in Public Life.

ICF is most noted for its Sarajevo Commitment, a statement of best practice which journalists and other media professionals are encouraged to adhere to. It was launched in 2000, after a Bosnian Muslim radio journalist invited Porter to organize an ICF event in Sarajevo. Senad Kamenica had been incensed by the reporting bias of local Bosnian Serb and Croat journalists, which in his view had whipped up ethnic tensions prior to the outbreak of the Balkans war of 1992-1995. Some had been prepared to lie for their side, Kamenica said, and he believed their behaviour had 'contributed to more deaths than weapons had'.

The Sarajevo Commitment has been the ICF's only published

declaration of best practice and is nothing if not inspirational: 'We shall combine freedom with responsibility, talent with humility, privilege with service, comfort with sacrifice and concern with courage,' it reads in part. 'We realize that change in society begins with change in ourselves.'

Porter is keen that the ICF avoids any endorsement of censorship. Media professionals exchange their experiences at the forums, with the aim of encouraging each other to reflect for themselves on the balance between freedom and responsibility in the media. He maintains that the best guide to professional responsibility is the conscience: 'that remarkable piece of high technology that is inside us, albeit often covered over with the compromises of a lifetime, but which enables us to choose right from wrong, truth from falsehood'.

The Sarajevo Commitment, translated into 17 languages, has made a considerable impact. Jay Rosen, professor of journalism at New York University, compared it with Lincoln's Gettysburg Address, and declared that he would use it with all his students, while the former BBC newsreader Martyn Lewis became another keen advocate. Others have been more sceptical about its overt idealism. But Roger Parkinson, President of the World Association of Newspapers, commented that the ICF 'has put the issue of the effects of the media on society on the global agenda'.

The BBC's former war correspondent, Martin Bell, says that Bill Porter is 'an inspirational figure, and the moving spirit behind the Sarajevo Commitment of September 2000, which set out a much needed declaration of principles for journalists. It was in that city during the Bosnian War that we came to understand that we did not just reflect, but affect, the world around us. We had responsibilities as well as rights. The Sarajevo Commitment is the best statement of those realities that I know.'

Porter was born in 1920 on a farm in an East Anglian village and grew up in Lancashire. At Liverpool University, his search for a spiritual base in life was 'backed into second place by my devotion to worldly success and pretty girls', he wrote. He served as a lieutenant during World War II, in North Africa,

Italy and India, where he was a signals officer with the 17th Indian Infantry brigade. His experience there gave him a life-long love of India.

After the war he worked for a spell with Moral Re-Armament, but broke with the movement over a disagreement about aims and tactics. But he also admits that he found MRA's emphasis on sexual morality 'very restrictive and I was looking forward to my freedom in that respect'. Peter Howard, a Beaverbrook newspaper columnist who became MRA's leader, told Porter: 'You are meant to be a mighty tree, under whose branches many people can find shelter and purpose.' It was to be 35 years before Howard's vision for Porter began to be realized through the ICF.

Porter spent three years as a freelance journalist, including reporting on Tito's Yugloslavia, where he ended up in the Croatian port of Rijeka. His city guide and interpreter was an attractive red-haired woman, Sonja Aleksic. Her Bosnian mother was from an aristocratic background while her father, a Montenegran, was a colonel. 'My priorities steadily shifted away from the pursuit of the story to the pursuit of the lady,' Porter wrote. They were married in 1962.

Sonya was made of stern stuff, having been twice sentenced to death in her late teens and early 20s, first under the occupying Nazis, and then under the Yugoslav communist regime for being 'an enemy of the people'. So accused, she prepared herself for nine nights running to face death by firing squad. On the tenth morning she was suddenly released, thanks, she believed, to the influence of a Jewish friend who was an official in the Belgrade city government.

These traumatic experiences gave her a fierce independence of spirit. 'To survive such an experience without bitterness, to keep an open heart and a positive and cheerful outlook is a triumph of the human spirit,' Porter writes in his memoires, describing his nearly 30 years with Sonja as 'the deepest experience of my life'.

Bringing her to London after their marriage, he became the Marketing Director for John Grant's Eurobooks Ltd. This involved travelling to bookshops and universities all over Europe. But when Grant gave Porter the sack, largely over a misunderstanding, it led to his lucky break, being taken on by Kluwer.

Not everyone can say, as Porter does, that the 15 most fulfilling years of their lives began at 70. The tragic death of his wife, due to undiagnosed hepatitis, had been the spur. A large, bluff and jovial man, he likes to describe himself, in his journey towards a faith, as a 'lapsed agnostic'. Reflecting on the ICF, he says, 'When I decided to take this road, I experienced a sense of inner compulsion that has never left me. Where does it come from, if not from some superior guiding force in the universe?'

www.icforum.org

1. Bill Porter, *Do something about it: a media man's story,* published by John Faber, 2005

16

Business of change

*When the whole context in which you have existed changes,
what do you do? The Managing Director of a family firm
describes his experience.*

OUR FAMILY firm was founded by my great-great-grandfather in
the early 19th century. My forebears had a strong Christian
ethos, and this had significant consequences for the company
when, in the 1930s, my grandfather accepted the challenge to let
the Methodist faith, which he proclaimed and practised on a
Sunday, affect the way he ran the company from Monday to
Saturday.

His first idea was to go back into the factory with his eyes
open as if he were a stranger. He saw, for the first time, the
men's real working conditions. There were no washing facilities. There was no canteen. The yard was dirty. There was no
sick pay. There was little or no pension provision.
So, in an experiment of faith, he began to change these things.
He built washing and canteen facilities, introduced sick pay and
persuaded all the shareholders to give some of their capital to
set up a fund for the benefit of employees and their dependants.
During the Depression he deliberately created work and took
on staff.

This experience convinced my grandfather and father that
what was morally right was economically viable. Over the next
60 years, the business achieved worldwide success based on

quality, reliability, integrity and service. They saw the firm as a model for how relations between shareholders, management and employees could be, a working example of an alternative to industrial conflict and class war.

I came into the business straight from university, with various unspoken, and even unconscious, assumptions. Among these were:

- that life would go on for our company and for me as it had done before;
- that there would always be a business to run, markets to support us and a job for life for everybody employed in the company;
- that change would only come in small, incremental and digestible amounts;
- that we shareholders were meant to be stewards, not entrepreneurs.

After 12 years in the firm, I became Managing Director, responsible for the day-to-day running of the company. Over the next three years, sales increased and exports grew until we achieved our highest ever level of sales and of profit. But two years later we had our first recorded loss in over 70 years. Over the next four years our home market collapsed and export markets shrank as customers moved their production to countries where we could not compete.

In responding to this business crisis, our company went through four stages: denial, coping, positive acceptance and planning.

We were slow to realize that this was more than just another cyclical downturn, albeit a pretty deep one, and that business was leaving our traditional markets in Europe for good. As a result of that denial we waited too long before we began to implement changes.

Coping involved having to reduce our workforce by about a quarter: a huge shock, both corporately and individually. We also brought all the employees together on one site which helped to improve communication and change the culture of the company. At the same time there was a transition of generations, as seven of the nine directors and three senior managers retired, and a new management team took their place. Then we accepted that, rather than having reached a new equilibrium, change was going to continue. This positive acceptance of change led us to switch the emphasis of our business into new fields. Many of our staff had to learn new skills: they have done so enthusiastically and with great success.

These responses were all essentially reactive; we had been managing change. But the time comes when you have to move from managing change to leading change. This required me to take active responsibility for our future.

As I was told on a training course, 'The only way to transform your company is to transform yourself.' I had to address attitudes which undermined my ability to be entrepreneurial: my tendency to feel a victim of circumstances, to prefer to avoid things rather than confront them, my fears, my aversion to risk-taking. I had to become willing to break rules, customs, precedents, assumptions and expectations which I had previously accepted as givens.

This fourth, planning, stage involved developing a long-term plan, making a fresh statement of the values which matter to us, developing new products, and identifying a whole new direction and technology for the company to adopt.

After the collapse of communism, the purpose which had inspired my father and grandfather lost some of its force for me: it no longer seemed relevant to talk about our company as a model of an answer to class war. But through the development of new, environmentally adapted and biodegradable products, a new sense of purpose began to emerge, around the idea of sustainability, which makes sense in the context of today.

This idea of sustainability implies long-term economic viability; relationships of trust and integrity both inside and outside the firm; satisfied staff who enjoy their work; and products and processes which do not denude or damage the environment.

In recent years, our company's markets have changed; our products have changed; our locations have changed; our structures have changed; our people have changed. I expect that we will be radically different again in five years' time. But what I have learnt, above all else, is that change really does start with me.

The writer asked to remain anonymous.
First published in For A Change magazine, December 2006.

17

Eight steps towards a values-centred leadership

What forensic evidence can we detect from examining these stories?
What clues do they yield? What qualities of leadership
do the people in these stories demonstrate?

THE STORIES in this book point to some of the qualities needed for successful leadership. Leadership can, of course, be bad or good: autocratic or inspirational. For leaders to be effective they have to carry people forward. Leadership also implies 'follow-ship'—a wholehearted willingness to go in the direction that the leader sets. Leadership has to engender trust.

Good leadership, then, is not just a question of power or authority, residing for instance in the boardroom. Nor is it simply a top-down, command structure of telling people what to do—though a good leader accepts responsibility, and may have to make unpopular or revolutionary decisions, risking being proved right or wrong by results. The acclaimed Brazilian entrepreneur Ricardo Semler provides an interesting example of a new style of leadership. He has written books about his company's 'flat'—as opposed to a vertical or centralized—leadership structure. He set in place a revolutionary, egalitarian workplace democracy, liberating staff to take initiatives in achieving company goals.[1] It seems to have worked for him. His company of 5,000 employees, Semco, has seen turnover grow from $40 million to over $1 billion.

There are many qualities of leadership, including vision, responsibility, attention to detail, delegation, sacrifice and service—and many books have been written about the nature and qualities of 'servant leadership'[2]. Leadership also embraces a love for people and, in this era of environmental awareness, a concern for future generations and the safety of the planet.

So what can be learnt about leadership from the experiences of the people in this book? Students of business ethics might find it an interesting exercise to review the stories in the light of this question. I detect from them eight steps to a values-centred leadership. These steps may not be comprehensive but they are essential to effective leadership.

1. They have *a vision and purpose beyond the bottom line*. None of the people in these stories have put making money or even profit as their first priority, however important profit is to their enterprise. They have shown a motivation beyond self-interest. Maximizing the return to shareholders and 'doing what is right for me'—too often today's mantra—have been transcended by doing what is right for the wider good. There is, of course, satisfaction in having a sense of purpose and meaning in life rather than accumulating wealth, even if this is a byproduct. But some people in these stories have made considerable self-sacrifices, foregoing higher incomes or the ladder of personal success for the sake of a greater purpose.

2. They encompass *a social dimension*, motivated by a social consciousness. Corporate social responsibility has become a fashionable mantra. The people in these stories have put it into practice. They have included community-building, job creation, environmental awareness, sustainability and notions of social justice as part of their commitment.

3. They show *a profound commitment to personal integrity*. Company founders and CEOs can, of course, set the ethical agenda, their values permeating the companies they run. Tata's social ethos, for instance, is thanks to the vision of the com-

pany's founding pioneer, Jamshetji Tata, who was one of the giants of Indian industry. None of the people in this book claim to be paragons of virtue, and all would admit to making mistakes. But they have all held on to core moral and ethical values in their lives and businesses, including the courageous stance against corruption.

Consciously or innately, the people in this book have aspired to the qualities of integrity listed by Roger Steare in his book *Ethicability*: prudence, justice, fortitude, temperance, trust, hope, love, excellence, and respect[3]. Many of the people quoted have also found strength in the moral and ethical values of Initiatives of Change, including honesty, purity of heart and motive, selflessness and detachment, a love for people, a sense of forgiveness and the search for wisdom. These values have encouraged their commitment to transparency and trustworthiness.

4. They have built ***relationships of trust***, whether between management and labour or between boardroom members; between those of privilege and those who have been dispossessed; between companies and customers; between sectors of the community; and in family relationships. As Ward Vandewege in Boston emphasizes, relationships of trust are essential for business survival.

5. They have been ***prepared to take risks***: to go out on a limb. They have taken courageous business and career decisions, including taking bold investment decisions, developing new products, or even turning down lucrative positions. Some have also risked relationships with friends and colleagues. In at least one case this led to a parting of the ways. They have gone through the barrier of fear of what others might think of them, including the fear of ridicule. In so doing they have found themselves knocking on open doors. Bill Porter, for instance, found that he was tapping into a groundswell of support, and was even prophetically ahead of the game in tackling what Tony Blair years later called the 'feral beast' of the media.

6. They have shown **singleness of purpose**. The people in these stories have not been distracted by lesser aims. Like William Wilberforce and his company of 'Clapham saints', who campaigned in the British parliament for 20 years to abolish the slave trade, they have each kept their eye on the long-term goal; they have dug in for the long haul. None pretended that their lives and tasks would be easy or involve quick-fix solutions. But they have surmounted difficulties. As the Mumbai businessman Suresh Vazirani told me, 'Every difficulty becomes an opportunity.' The people in this book have shown a set of the will which has seen them endure hardship and set-backs, but they have fought through them and, in enduring, have won.

7. They have **developed leadership teams around them**, rather than relying on their own skills. In some cases they have pulled out of pre-eminent roles in order to encourage growth in others and a new leadership. Charlotte Bannister-Parker and Sophia Swire built up a powerful board of committed trustees before resigning from the leadership of their educational charity. Bill Porter and his colleagues have expanded the International Communications Forum into a series of national chapters with local leaderships.

8. They have found **inspiration in spiritual resources and silent reflection**. For some this has meant a belief in a divine presence and purpose. One psychologist's definition of motivation is 'all those pushes and prods—biological, social and psychological—that defeat our laziness and move us, either eagerly or reluctantly, to action'. Not all moral conviction comes from religious sources. But those pushes and prods can also be inspirational, from the wellsprings of spiritual, religious and ethical inputs. In his book *Building a better world*, Malcolm Duncan writes about 'the role of motivational factors in changing society'. One of these, he says, is faith which, he argues, has 'a very important place in the public square'. 'Our faith can help us to shape or to understand our own values… We cannot exclude faith from shaping our engagement in our societies. To do so is to remove at least one lung from individuals.'[4]

The people in this book have each followed a calling in life driven forward by such an inner impulse. And their journeys have been as important as their destinations. Far from the ends justifying the means, their means—including integrity, relationships of trust and the search for revealed truth in times of silent reflection—have shaped, even determined, their ends. They have each been guided by a light, not always knowing where it would lead but surprised, perhaps even delighted, by the road it has revealed.

The stories in this book are far from unique. There are many others like them. Ray Anderson, the former CEO of Interface, the world's largest carpet maker, is known as 'America's greenest chief executive'. He talks about his 'epiphany moment' when he read Paul Hawken's book *The ecology of commerce*[5]. The book was 'like a spear to the chest', he said, inspiring him to make his company environmentally friendly, at a time when it was producing nearly 900 pollutants. This coincided with feedback from customers and employees concerned about the company's impact on the environment. He took steps to reduce waste and conserve energy through recycling. 'It's not just the right thing to do, it is the smart thing to do,' he said. Profits increased and he declared: 'The new course we're on at Interface… is to pioneer the next industrial revolution: one that is kinder and gentler to the earth.'[6]

Another pioneer is the software and website entrepreneur Bela Hatvany who founded Silverplatter, the world's first company to put information onto CD-Rom. It included medical reference information for researchers. After he sold the business he funded two Internet companies, www.justgiving.com and www.firstgiving.com, where individuals can donate to their favourite charitable causes. Every day 20,000 people donate an average of $50, or a million dollars a day, 'and it is still growing like topsy', he says. 'Gratitude and acceptance are my twin watchwords,' he adds. He likens 'spiritual information', gained in times of silent reflection, to 'the central nervous system which allows the body of human-kind to function'. This, he says, is what has inspired him in his business initiatives.

Pamela Hartigan, Managing Director of the Schwab Foundation for Social Entrepreneurship in Geneva, says that social entrepreneurs 'have a mission of transformational social change'. They are 'what you get when you combine Richard Branson and Mother Teresa—a hybrid between business and social value creation'[7]. The Ashoka foundation, founded by Bill Drayton in the USA, has a similar mission 'to shape a citizen sector that is entrepreneurial, productive and globally integrated', developing social entrepreneurship around the world. Ashoka identifies and invests in leading social entrepreneurs— 'extraordinary individuals with unprecedented ideas for change in their communities'. Over 1,800 Ashoka Fellows are given professional support and access to a network of peers in over 60 countries.[8] Hartigan says that such social entrepreneurs 'need imaginative, compassionate and talented people from all sectors to help them to live up to their promise.'[9] Those quoted in this book would agree.

Adam Smith wrote *The Theory of Moral Sentiments*. The people whose stories are told here have put moral sentiment into practice. The qualities of leadership and inspiration they show, and the ethical and spiritual resources they draw on, have helped to change the world.

1. See especially his book *Maverick*, Random House, 1993.

2. The Amazon website reveals some 70 books addressing the subject.

3. *Ethicability*, Roger Steare Consulting Limited, 2006, pp 35-36

4. *Building a better world: faith at work for change in society*, Malcolm Duncan, Continuum, London, 2006, p 37. Rev Malcolm Duncan is the head of Faithworks in the UK. www.faithworks.info

5. *The ecology of commerce: a declaration of sustainability*, Paul Hawken, 1994

6. Anderson was appointed co-chair of President Bill Clinton's Sustainable Development Council in 1997 and was named Entrepreneur of the Year by Ernst & Young. I am indebted to an article by Jennifer Beck for this information.

7. 'Everybody's business', *For A Change* magazine, April/May 2006

8. www.ashoka.org

9. Hartigan, *Everybody's business*

Postscript

THE STORIES presented here are a mere selection. Most of them are people I know through a common involvement with the international programme of Initiatives of Change (IofC), which aims to build 'relationships of trust across the world's divides'. IofC includes Caux Initiatives for Business (CIB) which runs regular conferences at IofC's global conference centres in Caux, Switzerland, and Panchgani, India. Some of the people in this book are involved in IofC's Farmers Dialogue programme.

CIB aims to encourage trust, integrity and leadership. Its mission is to 'strengthen the motivations of care and moral commitment in economic life and thinking in order to create jobs, correct economic and environmental imbalances and address the root causes of poverty'. CIB aims to 'equip people with practical tools, grounded in a moral and ethical framework, for use in their places of work. The forums are motivated by a mutual commitment to address economic problems of immediate or long-term concern, including environmental imbalances, poverty, corruption and social exclusion.'

The Farmers Dialogue encourages farmers worldwide to 'think globally—act locally' and to 'renew their calling to feed the world'. One of its aims is 'to help farmers see themselves as an immediate road out of poverty for their communities'.

I wanted to present these stories in the hope that they would be a source of inspiration to others, particularly to those setting out in the early stages of their careers.

www.iofc.org
www.cauxbusiness.org
www.farmersdialogue.org

Acknowledgements

MANY THANKS to all the people whose stories appear in this book and who have spoken so frankly about their experiences. My thanks also go to those who have written some of the chapters: John Bond, Garfield Hayes, Joseph Karanja, Ron Lawler and the anonymous contributor, who have kindly allowed me to reproduce their stories. Many thanks go, too, to Blair Cummock, the typographic designer, Hayden Russell who designed the cover and my publisher at Caux Books, Andrew Stallybrass. A number of people have given me valuable advice, ideas and perspectives for the book including Mohan Bhagwandas, John Carlisle, Chris Evans, Sarosh Ghandy, Mark Perera, Peter Rundell, Christoph Spreng, Stephen Young and David and Elizabeth Locke. That said, any errors are mine. My thanks also go to the Irene Prestwich Trust which gave me a grant towards research for the book. And, of course, many thanks to my wife, Jan, for all her encouragement and support.

Michael Smith, July 2007

Bibliography

Miles Davis, *Planet of slums*, Verso, 2006

Malcolm Duncan, *Building a better world: faith at work for change in society*, Continuum, 2006

Al Gore, *An inconvenient truth*, Rodale Books (USA), 2006, Bloomsbury (UK), 2006

Paul Hawkin, *The ecology of commerce: a declaration of sustainability*, HarperBusiness, 1994

Christopher Jamison, *Finding sanctuary: monastic steps for everyday life*, Phoenix, 2007

R M Lala, *The Creation of Wealth*, Penguin Books India, 2004

Edward Luce, *In spite of the gods: the strange rise of modern India*, Little, Brown, 2006

P J O'Rourke, *On the wealth of nations*, Atlantic Books, 2007

Bill Porter, *Do something about it: a media man's story*, John Faber, 2005

Jeffrey Sacks, *The end of poverty*, Penguin Books, 2005

Ricardo Semler, *Maverick*, Random House, 1993

David Smith, *The dragon and the elephant: India, China and the new world order*, Profile Books, 2007

Roger Steare, *Ethicability*, Roger Steare Consulting, 2006

Joseph Stiglitz, *Globalization and its discontents*, Penguin Books, 2002; *Making globalization work*, Penguin Books, 2006

Stephen Young, *Moral capitalism*, Berrett-Koehler Publishers, 2003

Michael Smith *is a freelance journalist working with Initiatives of Change, the international body which aims to build relationships of trust across the world's divides. He is a co-ordinator in Britain of Caux Initiatives for Business (CIB), one of the programmes of Initiatives of Change.*

He served on the newsweekly magazine Himmat in Mumbai, India, for three years in the 1970s. Returning to Britain he joined the editorial staff of The Industrial Pioneer, which published his first book, Beyond the Bottom Line. In 1987 he became one of the founding editors of For A Change magazine, published by Initiatives of Change in London, a position he held for 18 years. He is the author of the booklet The Sound of Silence which has been translated into several languages. His articles have appeared in national newspapers, including The Financial Times, The Guardian, The Independent, The Times, Sunday Business and The Herald, Scotland. He is also an honorary member of the Texas-based International Association of Obituarists.

He and his wife Jan live in Wimbledon and they have two children.